Manifest West

Women of the West

Manifest West

Women of the West

WESTERN PRESS BOOKS
GUNNISON, COLORADO

Western
Press Books

ISBN: 978-1-60732-726-4

Library of Congress Control Number: 2017932060
Published in the United States of America

Western Press Books
Gunnison, Colorado

Cover image: ISTOCKPHOTO.COM

"Manifest" by Kierstin Bridger was previously published in *All Ember* (Urban Farmhouse Press, 2016).

"Homesteading in Paradise" by Sally Clark was previously published in *Relief: A Quarterly Christian Expression Journal*, Volume 1, Issue 1 (ccPublishing NFP, 2006).

"When She Speaks," ". . . Treasure," ". . . Empty Spaces," and ". . . Rosewater" by Harrison Candelaria Fletcher first appeared in *Ghost Town* (Issue 8, Fall 2015), and are reproduced from *Presentimiento: A Life in Dreams* with permission from Autumn House Press. Copyright © 2016 by Harrison Candelaria Fletcher.

"The Swallows" by Rick Kempa was previously published in *High Desert Journal* (Ryder Graphics, Spring 2008).

"Grandma Sits Down" by Rick Kempa was previously published in *When I am an Old Woman* (Papier-Mache Press, 1987).

"My Galapagos" by Annie Lampman was previously published in *Talking River* (Associated Students of Lewis-Clark State College, 2004).

"A Mother's Guide to Birds and Boys" by Annie Lampman was previously published in *High Desert Journal* (Ryder Graphics, Spring 2014).

"If Women Ran the World" by Ellaraine Lockie was previously published online in *Triplopia* (2007).

"Witches of the West" by Ellaraine Lockie was previously published in *Sein und Werden* (ISMs Press, 2006).

"The House on Willamette Falls Drive" by Scot Siegel was previously published in *The Constellation of Extinct Stars and Other Poems* (Salmon Poetry, 2016).

STAFF

EDITOR
Caleb Seeling

CONSULTING EDITOR
Mark Todd

ASSOCIATE EDITORS
Sapphire Heien
Sheena Feiler
Elizabyth A. Hiscox

ASSISTANT EDITORS
Zoe Henderson
Levi Larson
Bella Lewis
Douglas Nelson
Brett Nielsen
James Powell IV
Kennedy Sievers
Jay Ytell

DESIGN & LAYOUT
Sonya Unrein

CONTENTS

Introduction   1

INHERITANCE

Kierstin Bridger
Manifest   5

Debbie Day
Moving West   7

David Lavar Coy
The Rancher's Third Marriage   8

Lisa Levine
Slut   9

Corinna German
A Woman Can   19

Paula Bramlett
Annie Oakley   22

Don Cadden
Cow Women   31

David Lavar Coy
The Navajo Woman   33

Robert Kostuck
Changing Woman   34

Ellaraine Lockie
If Women Ran the World   52

Leah Hedrick
Remnants, Pt. III   54

Riashantae Sides
Western Woman   55

Harrison Candelaria Fletcher
. . . Treasure   57

Ellaraine Lockie
Witches of the West   58

Anita Cruse
Sunflower Women   60

ALBUM

Carolyn Dahl
Emma's Seeds   65

Harrison Candelaria Fletcher
When She Speaks   66

David Lavar Coy
Grandma's Apron   67

Cindy L. Prater
My Vietnam Blessing   68

Gail Denham
Apron   72

Sally Clark
Homesteading in Paradise   73

Rick Kempa
A Circle of Family   76

Harrison Candelaria Fletcher
. . . Rosewater   79

Kathleen Winter
Mean Time, Prime Time   80

Carolyn Dahl
Boss Over the Bull   81

GUST

Annie Lampman
My Galapagos   85

Betsy Bernfeld
Bleeding in the Wilderness   86

Rick Kempa
The Swallows   89

Annie Lampman
A Mother's Guide to Birds and Boys   90

Harrison Candelaria Fletcher
. . . Empty Spaces   100

TORN

Gail Denham
Lonely Vigil in Colorado   103

Jessica McDermott
An Only Daughter Walks with Her Father   105

Lisa Levine
The Darkest   107

Don Kunz
An Incident at Big Sandy Creek, 1864   116

Rick Kempa
Grandma Sits Down   118

Scot Siegel
The House on Willamette Falls Drive   119

Paula Coomer
Basic Nostalgia   121

CONTRIBUTOR NOTES

Contributor Notes   130
About the Staff   135

Introduction

Those of us living in the West's mountains, plains, cities, and deserts can all bear witness that there is no one type of Western woman. They are cowgirls and office staff, rock climbers and birdwatchers, First Nations members and migrant workers. Some Western women no longer live here, instead looking back on the home they left behind, and others are recent immigrants from the East Coast or the Far East. What connects their identities is the sharing of Western ways of life: family, heritage, a complicated relationship with the land's utility and beauty. Meanwhile, issues universal to women everywhere—threats of physical violence, societal controls on their sexuality, and varied definitions of femininity—cannot be overlooked, for they also impact Western women. These ladies are individual squares of a quilt, and their interactions with the culture, landscape, and geography of the West, and with their families and each other, offer us a unified variety.

The editorial team of *Manifest West* is proud to offer a diversity of voices in this volume that celebrates Western women as an inclusive category, not a stark label. Both female and male authors and poets share their observations and interpretations. We explore the experiences of Hispanic, First Nations, and even Thai women of the West. Their narratives include mothers, daughters, straight women, gay women, and women whose stories refuse to be defined by romance and family, instead spotlighting their passions as hobbyists, workers, and *humans*.

This volume's thirty-seven poems, short stories, and creative nonfiction essays dialogue with each other on a myriad of subjects. We gathered them into four sub-categories to highlight their closest conversations, but we know you will still notice abundant crossovers between these distinctions.

"Inheritance" explores the impact of the old ways of the West on a woman today, along with the challenges all of womankind bear on their shoulders. Alongside a relatable rendering of Annie Oakley's life and Navajo transitions from generation to generation, you will find a schoolgirl confronting judgment for her sexuality and a protest cry against all-too-common violence against women.

In "Album," flip with us through the pages of ten family portraits. A daughter questions her father's dictate to lord oneself over livestock, a niece shares how her immigrant aunt's struggle for inclusion guided her own path to womanhood, and several women draw life lessons from their ancestors' kitchen aprons.

"Gust" leads us outside and into nature. A little girl discovers symbiotic compassion in animals, a grandmother demonstrates a respect for all life, even that which intrudes on our own, and a rock climber relates the challenges of taking on Mother Nature while existing as a fertile woman.

"Torn" depicts rifts and loss, the canyons in life that Western women find themselves struggling to climb out of. Daughters lose their fathers to death and to rejection, a caver grapples with the knowledge that the man she loves is tethered to another, and we pause to reflect on a mother's experience of an atrocious massacre.

Some of these stories and poems reinforce expectations, others overtly defy them, and many fall in the middle, all reflecting the diverse experiences that make up real life. These ladies, and so many more, are the women of the West.

INHERITANCE

KIERSTIN BRIDGER

Manifest

I am a child of HUD houses,
the cardiac arrest of the Rockies,
a child of sage and tumbleweed,
of living a sandstone's throw from the cemetery—
a frozen crust and moonboot trudge,
the dusty bike ride to the rodeo grounds,
the dare to walk across vast wooden beams
above splintered stadium seats.

I am a child of the 80s, of television, turning the silver knob
on the squat console, no '84 Olympics; the smashed
black-and-white against the drywall's corner bead—
a child of a Vietnam vet and a beauty school queen,
the grandchild of an Indian man whose mother skinned
more than knees on the Trail of Tears,
who sold her heritage for two beets and a warm chicken egg.

I am the mutt of Black Ireland,
dark veins and snake-handling Sundays,
of winding Kentucky hollers
and panthers who scream in the night—
moonshine feuds and bottles broken for scarring.
Folks who lived deep in the ivy of Appalachian mountains,
of mustard poultices, and honeycomb on the table for biscuits.

I am sanity's child who fled by rutted frontage roads
stained by black lung and bad luck,
who reached out to a man I didn't have to save because,
though I am the product of generations of teenage lust
and long highways of losing him in the rearview,
I'm also the daughter of women who work,
of deep grease in the folds of corporate uniforms.

I am a child of stocked pantries, aluminum canisters
of powdered milk and blocks of government cheese.
I am public education, taxed on the back of a mother
who cut hair for years, who fed countless strands
through two fingers under the florescent light
of a beat-up, post-war shack—
child of cottonwood and aspen,
who hand fished in the Arkansas.
My voice, crack and lightning strike
in the heart of piñon pine.

DEBBIE DAY

Moving West

We leave the East, with its swarming cities, dripping hot woods, and waterways. The wetness and green is squeezed out dry with every rotation of our minivan tires. We arrive at our new town, nestled under the Wyoming mountains. Endless yellow plains, parched and rocky. The silence carves a hole in my stomach for the wind to blow through. The neighbors tell me it's a great place to raise kids, though they keep to themselves. I take my children to the empty parks, barren walkways. Cactus grips the broken cement. We stare at the Platte River dug into the red rock. An owl swoops across the water that glistens against a decorated sunset like we've never seen the sky before. Pale sunrises whisper each morning, the smell of hollowness. Every day I wait for something I can't hear. The lost train bids goodbye, briefly passing through, entering into sand, brush, nothing. My husband loves it here. I wonder if we'll stay long. I think of fireflies in the East, the wall of beech trees curtaining the sky, the nosy old woman downstairs, the screams through the ceiling, waiting for Daddy as he sits in five rows of stagnant cars. Laugher awakens me. I look out the window at my children playing in the front yard. Beside the vacant road, they jump sprinklers and zig-zag with bicycles, garbed in dripping popsicles. A gush of air opens the door. An invitation. I step out to greet the strange quiet. A loneliness, a ghost from a distant memory, a peace I've never known.

DAVID LAVAR COY

The Rancher's Third Marriage

No dust on the seat of his pants,
his lip curled with tobacco and amusement.
He takes on another wife at fifty,
the last one *rode* too hard,
tamed into a routine slowness.

The new bride is tough as him,
having thrown her other lovers.
The old equation of love
adds up correctly—two who cherish
as one the same acres of scrub brush,

who pull garden weeds together—farm
and raise cattle—two in the fields
bailing hay, riding the trails horseback.
Determined to get love done right.
In their ranch house, the lights glow

and bugs bump against the windows.
They snuggle down under a quilted history,
ready, tomorrow, for anything.
I wish them a life peaceful as fishing,
but I know marriage will carry them

down hilly back roads like a truck
with worn gears and broken mirrors.

Slut

Note: As a story born of the border, "Slut" contains unitalicized Spanish as a representation of regional speech patterns.

From inside the ring of girls, Elisa darts out and slaps her. "Slut." Even the sting in María's eyes must be the mingling floral stink of their perfumes, because no tears break as she cuts a look towards Patrick. He stands apart, spinning skateboard wheels back and forth across his palm and saying nothing in her defense. "It wasn't my fault." Her mouth flattens into a sullen line. "He made me."

From beside Elisa, the victim on attack, another girl with blue-rimmed eyes shoves her face in María's, so close María can smell her minty, sour breath: "Mary Alvarez. You're so—" but the girl can't produce a word.

Instead another picks up: "It was the boys' bathroom."

"Apologize to her."

"You could have told him no, slut."

"Slut," chimes in the last, but the rest are pulling away, tossing hair over shoulders and bending to pick up backpacks. The fight is over, and the girls break apart as a distant bell reminds everyone of places they need go—Annex B, West Campus, P.E. fields. María waits for the others to disappear. Her thin cheeks burn as Patrick moves away, grabbing the board lengthwise and reaching for Elisa's hand. She waits, invisible again, as they run off, two this way, one that, the fight vanished save for her fists, balled too late, and her stinging cheek. Finally, she shoulders her backpack and starts to sprint toward the P.E. fields, passing Elisa and Patrick on her way. From behind she hears a falsetto echo: "Slut," followed by a high-pitched giggle.

By lunch, multiplying versions of what happened in the bathroom are written in selected eyes, girls from certain cliques, even growing, to—she swears—the quick glance of a young, frizzed-out Home Ec teacher. Anticipating another gauntlet of stares from around the cafeteria, María closes in on herself, sensing warmth beneath her worn pink t-shirt, girls size 14, every point of its yellow star decal as faded as her feelings. She ignores the dour slap of mashed potato against plastic as she passes through the line. Her backpack rubs diagonal red welts across her collarbone, so tightly clutched are its pair of straps to her body. After eating she walks across the cafeteria, head down; she is going home early today. "Cramps," she tells the nurse, who looks at her through blue plastic glasses, offended, María thinks, like the girls, like Nana would be. Everyone must see her as the slutcallers do, honest words forbidden in their small Mormon town. Even the old, gap-toothed front office aide who checks her dismissal pass smirks at her, licking his single incisor before initialing her out.

Intermittent rain falls all the way home from school, bursts that wet her hair and arms then disappear next block. Looking up at the sky between brief splatters, María walks down Far Street, past First Baptist and the EZ-Wash, conscious only of the rain and her feet, which she keeps moving. At her door, under a ray of patchy sunlight, she pauses to look at the empty porch next door. Between her yard and the neighbors' lies a bare dirt strip filled with puddles, a flood almost, with water running down the road where ruts now lurk underwater. At her door, her taut hands release the straps and her backpack slips to one hand, dangling at her side. She takes pleasure in slamming the swollen wood shut behind her, even though it will piss off Nana. Her anger lasts long enough for her to tear out a cola from the fridge pack and shove open the unscreened kitchen window, glaring where neighbor boys would be if this were after school. She can hear Nana bump into the squeaky bed frame in the back room. At the noise, María backs out of the kitchen, flops on the couch and finds the clicker. Too late, though—"Buenas, mija," says Nana, standing in slippers at the empty doorframe.

"Hi," she says, not looking away from the TV.

Together they watch the soap, caught up in the image of a matte-skinned brunette turning wide eyes towards the camera, lips quivering, the same longing for her lover in her face over and over in every frame and on every face. Her perfection becomes theirs by watching, María understands it; she's watched her grandmother get caught up in snippets of these her whole life. Nana's calm, but these women are forever in crisis—and watching, sprawled, feet up, skin sallowed by the fading light and electronic glow, María runs her hand through her hair where Patrick's had been a few days ago. At the time it was a clutching, unhurried request, how men and women talk. María. Her name was all it took. But she can imagine him with Elisa, too, his girlfriend in public, hands on her, keeping her close and telling her Mary Alvarez is *nothing. She just—she makes shit up.* A slut, a liar.

If María were prettier he'd be scared to say it. Beauty's terrifying. But Elisa isn't beautiful. Not to María. More that she's popular. Same thing.

Inside, it is sundown, almost, and no more rain is falling by the time Nana's telenovelas segue into a werewolf movie. Grateful to have vacated her thoughts, which have been swirling around the moment she stood facing Elisa, too shocked to react. María forgets about the slap, about the wildfire rumor that forced it to happen, until a harsh, exaggerated Latin insult—"Chinga tu hermana, cabrón"—snaps her head away from the television. She looks next door, where the guys are in each other's faces again, cigarettes dropping to the porch until someone sets a plastic cup back up on the railing and another digs into his pocket, holds his open palm out to the rest. María watches the boys' hands. The quarters are too thin to see from here, but she has played the game before. Everything about them, their tempers, their cigarettes, seems to suit a day like this, but before she can get up to borrow one, she hears their voices cut out, lowering, as the jingle of a key in the lock arrives at her front door. Her dad is lanky and loud—chains and motorcycle boots loud, not his voice, which is low and soft.

"Hey," she says.

"Hey," he glances up at her, still half on the phone. "Whatcha doin'?"

She looks at the TV and answers even if he isn't talking to her. "Who knows."

Miraculously, he clicks the phone shut. "Oh yeah?" Leans back out the front door and spits tobacco. "Must be watching something, if it's on."

"A movie."

"Huh." He heads back to his bedroom. Through the window María can see the game start up again, the boys settling back into their wicker chairs or along the wood railing, where the one she knows from school, Rico, is sitting. Through their sparkling front window, slanted with sunlight and air dust, she sees one of them turn in her direction. Can he see her? What's he heard? Better not stir.

"What the fuck's wrong with you?" Dad asks, stripped to his t-shirt now, tall and broad, blocking the couch opposite her. "School called. You ditching?"

She almost glares back, but closes her eyes instead, *Use your words*, just like they told her right around when the state sent him home for good. *One, two, three, four* before looking at him. "I was on the rag, Dad, wanna see?"

His motorcycle boots clunk, his personal dialect of discontent. Like her, he speaks in code but doesn't give up. "Get yourself cleaned up?"

"Yes." Hair heavy in her face now, better than a curtain for hiding behind.

"Well." He gets up, walks to the door, jangling, pops it open, to lean out and spit again. "Let me know next time. Didn't know why they called."

María waits on the couch until she hears the back door shut. Dad will be out until dark, riding around town. On a different day she would follow him out there while he started up the bike and see about a ride to the QuikMart, but the idea of other people weights her mind—she can't walk past them, the bums, the shifties, the moms. When dinner time starts closing in, maybe she will slip out to sit with the boys, like she does sometimes with her girlfriends, perching on the porch railing until Nana comes out looking for her. She can win at their game, if she tries. She's good at flipping the heavy coins just so off her fingers, and doesn't care too much when they start to shift in their chairs or get up and mutter to each other. Either way, when she sits back at the end of her turn, their hands will end up on her, leaning forward, maybe, for a forceful toss.

Nana calls out from the back room but María can already hear her walking out as she lifts herself up on one elbow. "What?" she asks as her grandmother's stretched-long shadow crosses the screen. Really Nana is short; quick like a hummingbird.

"Te sientes bien?" Instead of answering, María looks outside again at Rico, who wears a dark sweatshirt with the sleeves cut off, his hair buzzed short. His is a face she has seen again and again, here and at school. He knows her—María, Mary—and the coins flip past to more laughter.

"I'm fine. I'm not sick," María says. As if on a string, she gets up and walks out to the side yard, where there's laundry with her shirts to pull from the line. She stares harder now that there's no window between them, but he doesn't look back until her head is bent over the stiff shoulders of dad's work shirt, folding, then unclipping the next.

"Doing your chores?"

She looks up, startled by the closeness of the husky voice, but the face is wrong. An older man, not the boy she knows from school, is watching her over the chicken-wire fence, hand resting on it as if it was a thing belonging to him. "I don't know," she tells him.

"Me either," he responds.

She shrugs and then stands up straight, preparing to walk away. "Bonita, pero joven," he says. She shrugs, not sure how to answer and backing away with the stiff bundle clutched over her chest. María's eyes can't help but drag over their porch, but from this angle the boys she'd been watching are out of sight. Was he looking? She knows he must have been. Hope for attention drags at her heels as she finally turns around and walks back inside, shadowy, like the feeling from when she first met Patrick away from school, an accident, because her dad worked for his mom. Maybe it was a work picnic or maybe just them, their families. There was the smell of charcoal and raw ground meat, there was wind all over the table and in her hair, there was the excitement of being watched in such a way that you know you are being seen all the way through, like a hollow earth. Patrick's mother worked two jobs. "Two?" María had asked.

She had sighed and rolled her eyes, yes. "My kids are teenagers, so . . ." she explained, turning to look at Patrick, her boy, as he walked to the lake's edge. With sudden force his arm had swung out and flung a rock across the water.

María's dad had called out, "Hey, come get your burger," and Patrick came and sat next to María. When the others were busy with their meals, Patrick's hand crept across her leg, under the table, and stopped. She looked down and there it was, a little scarred at the knuckles, as familiar and solid as the handle of her screen door against her palm.

The memory settles, and she slips back inside her house, leaving the shirts on the arm of the couch and flipping the pages of her biology book. Her eyes trace sentences without remembering their meanings. After a page, she goes back outside and walks up the front lawn to where the boys are.

"Hey," she says to the boy she knows, twisting her hair and ignoring the others.

He glances, then sees her. "Wow, I didn't even hear you coming."

"I'm quiet," María says. "Like a cat." His face reddens and he picks at the railing with one finger. "Do you have a cigarette?"

"I don't smoke, but he does," he says, pointing at one of the others. Up close, she can see the others aren't boys but men, and maybe it was that way before but she didn't notice because she was there with another girl. María waits while the man passes over a cigarette, saying something she doesn't catch, and when the boy thumbs the lighter for her she backs away.

"I'll have it later," she says. "Thanks." María can think of a million places to smoke, like by one of the cottonwoods or in the wash behind their house, but instead she hides the cigarette in her makeup bag.

That night, she falls asleep on the couch, waking up very late at night to the sound of her father closing the screen door, and with channel numbers two and six ground into her thigh from the remote. "Ow," she says, sitting up.

Dad stops, and for a sleep-laden second she expects him to put his hand on her shoulder and point her to her bed, where she can slip between clean sheets and piles of discarded shirts and sweaters and plastic bracelets. Instead he tells her, "I didn't even see you there." María sinks inside, curling back to face the inner cushions, ignoring the hollow clack of his chain belt against the doorframe as he walks into the kitchen.

The next morning, María walks to school, sleepy still and dragging her boots along the sidewalk. They have fake brown fur coming out the tops. Her legs are bare above them, warm already, but she still wears the boots, which come up to just below her knees and will make her toes sweat by third period. She can see the boy, her cigarette brother, walking to school behind her. Waiting for him seems indecent, an assumption, but not waiting seems rude, so she looks back and smiles at him. His hand gives a little wave, inadvertent, the way she would touch her hair. But he catches up to her at the light without saying anything, just comes up beside her at the end of Far and walks Main at her side, almost splitting off when they get to the parking lot, where his friends wait. "Hey," María says as he starts to jog away.

He turns back and bobs his chin, *what*?

She tries to smile at him, corners of her lips buckling almost to break, uncertain what he thinks of her. "So, tell me, what did you hear about me? It's okay," she laughs, almost, shaking her head, lank strands falling back on her narrow shoulders, hands smoothing down the skirt, too short, too tight. "You can tell me."

He looks dead at her.

María squirms. "What? You can tell me."

His eyes drift to the side, lidded, and he tells her, "I don't talk." Then, pointing back at something on the road they've just walked, "You see that roof? We climbed it, my brother and I did, but he's too fat now to climb a roof. Not me though, I can run a four-forty mile."

María tosses her hair again, an unconscious, jerky parody of the confidence with which Elisa had tossed hers after slapping her in the face. He's afraid of me, she thinks, but before a response forms on her lips the thought of Patrick flashes in a blot of wordless shards, *afraid* and *me* and *boy* melting together in her mind far away from her sealed lips. Instead of answering the boy she smiles, sly like Patrick when he stopped her outside the unlocked cafeteria gate, his hand on hers, *what, me?* a nervous laugh, *The bathroom, the boys'? Why?* but his hand still in hers, popular, sexy Patrick, like summer hail, not possible but true, "María," he said, years of Spanish classes knotted up into his mouth.

"Me?" she said, and he shrugged, as if it were obvious all along, and then she saw inside him, alone in his arrogant body, his obvious need for her, now, his foot propped against the restroom door with the faint odor of urine fading in and out as she went to him and his fingers linked through hers. Patrick had pushed her up against the tile wall, his arms elbows-out like chicken wings, while she sank beneath his weight.

"I love this school," he told her. "You know how much I love this school?"

In her silence, her neighbor has melted back into the mess of bodies outside Building A. María stops at the fringes of even the ragged uncertain groups of kids, the memory of Patrick's embrace a brief, open window, clean and bright and unforgiving. The bells ring and she starts walking along the lockers in skittering, constrained steps. Still the sensation of him lingers, strained for clarity until her arms and hair and neck contain only the feeling of being loved, even as precise images of Patrick's body splash into nothing, rain hitting the pavement like scatters of lost water.

See, she wants to say to all the hard hallway eyes. *See what you've done.*

That night, at home, the porch next door stays empty while María paints her nails red, stroke by careful stroke. Nana sits with her for a little while, admiring her by lamplight. "Very nice, mija," she says. "You should, I think, always wear red. Is it your favorite color?" María shrugs, and the brush wobbles, marking her fingertip with a bright, sparkling wound. Her hand stings and then dries as she cleans the mistake in decisive swipes, like Nana at the windows. She uncaps the tiny bottle of red polish a second time as Dad comes back from out, cool and shaking off the night air, but by the time Nana lifts her hand to show him his daughter's nails, his eyes have already gone hard.

"Really?" he says. "You're trampin' it up now, too?"

*

The paved curbs stop where the numbers start. Patrick follows them, heading west, pushing off hard and steering through the numbered streets, down by Far where María lives. In his mind the echo of a door slams shut and he can hear his mom's outraged cry. The road beneath his board is balled up with wet gravel. He takes the last turn, trips, catches the board, skips a step and gets back on his wheels, smooth enough, with no one watching. Patrick's body, like elastic, expands to fit the emptiness of these streets. Movement drugs him, like his zombie friends at a game console, but he's better than all those fuckers, he's in motion while they sit back and react. He's all over the road, zigging back and forth around cracks and cutting turns dead middle, even the homeless dude would be watching if this was a normal town with homeless people out to watch the lucky ones live around them. He feels steady now. Only alone does he think of Mary, María, how she lets you touch her without response, lets you tell her what to do and lets you sit back and wait for her to do it.

Patrick dips off the corner, wails through a long, slick trail of water, skids to a stop. The yard is empty. He has never been here before on his own. He jiggles his foot, hand back in his pocket, when his back shudders under a fist.

He chokes out a breath and turns around to see a tall, dark-haired guy swinging at his ear. Patrick ducks, squares off. Peripherally he can see other faces, older. The boy rises up, bouncing almost, and Patrick lowers his body and rushes in to tackle him. They lurch across the street as one, legs tangling, falling into the gutter, the other pulls away and punches his face, concrete banging his head back, looks up at the rest, watching, their faces unreadable. *The boy, Rico, from fifth grade, maybe? A pickup game?* He stands up and kicks Patrick in his side. *Fuck this.* Patrick grabs his foot and thrusts him off balance, they are both down. Up on one elbow now, Patrick shakes off, jumps on top of the taller boy, starts pounding. The others' faces gather in closer, but the boy twists out and scuttles away, kicks at Patrick, hitting his ribs. "Thriller" starts to play and Patrick realizes it's his phone. "Hold up, man," he says. "It's my mom."

The older one steps out. "You just tell him stop?"

Patrick looks up from the square piece of metal he has pulled from his pocket. "Nah, just—no." He puts his hands down, signaling submission.

The man is in close, fast, his body short and thick. His breath in Patrick's face, boozy, like a day full of beer and talk. He says, "If he wants to fight you, you fight." He grabs the phone out of Patrick's hand and hurls it at the concrete, and when it bounces, still chanting out a tinny series of notes, he unbuckles his belt, grabs his dick, and pisses on the phone. It's a sloppy job, and the stream of urine strays towards Patrick's shoe. The canvas tongue goes warm, but he doesn't move his foot for fear what the guy will do next. In the distance a motorcycle guns rapid-fire. Patrick makes eye contact with the kid, who kind of shrugs as he steps over the piss puddle, kicking the phone away into the street.

"Just stay the fuck away from María," he says. "She thinks you talking shit."

Patrick's urge to kick his shoe off surges through his mouth instead. "Really? I didn't know you all called her that." The board is further out in the street, flipped up, and he eyes it for escape. If the wheels were down he'd grab it and take off.

The boy who started the fight doesn't say anything back, and the man, hands round over his belly, says only, "Do what he says." On the way back through the unlit streets to his house, where he is probably grounded until forever, this time, Patrick passes two leaned-back cruiser bikes, one with a woman clutching the driver's waist with her hair whipping out behind him.

The angry stutter of their motors rules the road, drowning out the murmur of his wheels on concrete long after the bikes are out of sight.

In the morning, the boy who jumped him will look for the phone on his walk to school. He will knock Patrick around again and again in his mind, turning the memory over and over until heat builds inside his chest and he can ignore his boring first-period geometry teacher. Her questions never have answers as certain as body meeting his fist. Later, in the cafeteria, his friends will all know how it went down, just as they know everything else about each other—one person tells a story, and then another, and the world crumbles and rebuilds. *Look*, he will say to María. *Look, just don't do it again.*

*

At the cafeteria doors, María remembers to smile. She feels better today, more natural, with her nails and lipstick and the borrowed cigarette stashed in her bag. She crosses the cafeteria with her head on high, faces turning, ignoring, no big deal, stops before her neighbor, glancing over his close-cropped hair. "I don't know what to say," she tells him, very quiet. Then she waits.

He shrugs. "I don't like that guy." His voice is also low, for her ears only. "I don't like him, but you. . ." He looks her up and down. Her lanky hair, her child-sized clothing, the nail polish, even, not the color but the fact that color is there, shiny. But she puts a hand on his palm, warm like a quarter begging to be tossed.

"It's okay," she says. "I know him, from before, it's—" She trails off, repeats, "I knew him from my dad."

"We all do," he says. Then, "María." Her name, is all.

Walking back to class, arms loose at her sides, María hears it again, "Slut."

"No I'm not," she fires back at the crowd. "I'm not a slut, he lied." Around her people disperse the same as before, scattering to class, the door, what happened in the bathroom, a rumor, nothing more.

CORINNA GERMAN

A Woman Can

I doubt you can hold a modified Warrior Pose
in the sage
for thirty minutes
while two hundred head of elk pace nervously, twenty yards away
Calves roll comically through barbed wire fence
and only my eyes laugh
They have no idea I'm there, watching, waiting,
clutching a single-shot .308
Then
get shot at in pursuit of the black antlered herd bull
by road hunters, eager to take what you've painstakingly
stalked
They took him, that day
I bet you can't keep up with me as
I hike straight up the mountain
in the Absaroka Wilderness
ripe with grizzlies
Walking on top of their tracks,
I tread gingerly
across the hillsides, dug up by their claws
I smell them: heavy rot, drifting from the Elderberry bushes
A Mama grizzly charged my husband once
and his heartbeat changed for
a week
Mine's changed too, ever since these
mountains charged my soul
I doubt you can track a buck
in these hills
on hands and knees, face to the ground,
urgently searching for one more drop of blood
while the wild phlox distracts

Or
spend a week in a tent sleeping on late fall's
snowy ground
in the pursuit of Mule Deer
If you ever do, you must
pause to inhale the
scent of
perfect little pines,
a shade of green that
clover would envy—
standing straight,
in Custer-Gallatin National Forest
I know you can't
carry two flea-infested foxes
on your shoulders
fresh from the trap line
as only a worthy pard does
wearing insulated coveralls
affectionately dubbed
The Leroy Suit
Or
walk ten miles looking for horns, those
sun-lit antlers in the sagebrush
Sleep that night
brings dreams about walking another ten
in the Shoshone National Forest where
Arrowleaf balsamroot is like a yellow brick road
leading to elk horns and
mountainsides full of glittering gypsum,
Septarian Nodules and
metal arrowheads, rusting away
In fall
near the Papy-Po Butte
I sit by a
cow's skull wedged

in the crook of a tree,
its bones a pile of tinker toys
holding my .300 Winchester—
a gun that the men say
is too big for a woman
In the next draw
The coyote clan howls and yips
while I turn my face to Wyoming's familiar wind
and walk on, to see what's moving down in the valley
knowing that a woman can

PAULA BRAMLETT

Annie Oakley

(1860-1926)

I lived my days dancing with contradictions. Born to parents who embraced the non-violent Quaker faith, I shot my way to fame with a rifle in
my hands. Raised in poverty, I dined with royalty. In seeking to defeat a
well-known marksman, I found, instead, my greatest ally. Sharing my bounty
with orphans, I remained childless. Living on the road among the sweat and
grit of rough men, I cultivated the serene elegance of a lady. And, at the end,
weary with the weight of travel, I found rest in the shadow of my childhood
home. Dancing with contradictions in a full, rich circle.

As often happens in families, my memories tangle with the stories of others.
I am intertwined with the story of the young Quaker girl, Susan Wise, and
her quiet Quaker man, Jacob Mosey. In 1848 they married, she sixteen and
he forty-nine, settling down right where they both started in Hollidaysburg,
Pennsylvania. And there they might have stayed if that fire hadn't happened
along, burning down their tavern and leaving them with no inn to keep.
Jacob, like so many others, wrapped his new beginning around the shine
of unbounded land to the west. Drake County, Ohio ended up looking like
home to Jacob and Susan. That's where the innkeepers became farmers and
that's where I came along, Phoebe Ann, the fifth Mosey girl, called Annie by
my sisters. After me a son, John, and another daughter.

With a sprawling family and a hard-scrabble farm, Jacob and Susan wrestled
with each day's grim shape. The two seemed to be holding their own until one
wintry time in 1866. After a hurried breakfast, Jacob stepped into the piercing
cold, his plan snug with certainty. Just taking in a load of wheat and corn to
be ground and, oh yeah, stopping for supplies on the way back. The hours
slipped by, casual at first, and then startling us with their long white quiet.
The blizzard caught hold of Jacob out there doing his chores and left an abid-
ing frost in his chest. He made his way home but didn't end up staying long.

Alone, with seven hungry mouths to feed, Mother wore herself to a shadow
fretting and scraping. We moved, renting a smaller place and she hired herself

out, birthing babies. But the hunger still tracked us down, stealthy as a fox slinking around a chicken house. At age eight, I concocted a scheme to help fill our empty stomachs. On that long stretch from Pennsylvania, Jacob had brought along a rifle, allowed by the gentle Quakers as a measure of protection against the dangers of the frontier. Hanging above our fireplace, it coaxed me to boldness. With John's help, I got it down and took my first shot. Small as I was, my aim hit the mark, true and clean. Our meals fattened up after that. Although Mother wondered how ladylike my new passion could possibly be, she didn't turn away the extra food. As for my own wonderings, from that first true shot to the last, I puzzled over the riddle of my untaught and unerring marksmanship.

Mother remarried. Soon after the birth of a daughter, she lost her new husband to an accident. The death of mother's helpmate, tied on to the arrival of another hungry young'un, threw our money-strapped family into a tailspin. I became cast-off weight.

I landed at the Drake County Infirmary, a place sheltering orphans, those down on their luck, and still others whose minds failed to wrap around simple tasks. The three-story building bulged with sad stories. The ones in charge, Samuel and Nancy Edington, ruled with kindness. I got to where I didn't mind so much.

If it hadn't been for those sneaky wolves coming around—that's what I called them for the rest of my days, "the wolves." Well, now, I better slow down on the blame and just stick to the facts. It started when that wolf in sheep's clothing slyly lured them all in with his earnest words and easy gait. A helper for his young wife, now, suddenly, a mother with a farmhouse to run. Yes, an able-bodied girl to shoulder some of the burden. He ended up saying all the right words, assuring school and wages. Mrs. Edington and mother both believed his honeyed promises. As for me, I watched the cunning wolf toss aside his sheep's clothing as soon as the infirmary disappeared in dust. Turns out the she-wolf waiting at the end of the trail happened to be meaner than spit, just like him. In two years' time I snuck out of the wolves' den, at twelve tired to the bone and battered as an old tin cup. The wolf put on his sheep's clothing and came to get me. But Mrs. Edington wasn't fooled this time, already having read the truth in the scars crossing my back.

Mrs. Edington kept me close after that. She figured out straightaway that those wolves didn't send me to school. In her brisk fashion she remedied the holes in my learning. Our lessons in reading, writing, and arithmetic lengthened into sewing and embroidery lessons as well. I found that my clever fingers could tease beauty out of ordinary cloth. This handy skill stuck with me for the rest of my days, my homemade show costumes a jumble of fanciful florals and swirls. You might say Mrs. Edington stuck with me too. We crossed letters through years of changes, the ones both great and small.

The infirmary seemed a settling place, until one day during my fourteenth year when a sudden longing for home startled my peace. I headed that way. Mother, now married to Joseph Shaw, labored through the wearying days on their twenty-seven-acre farm. While making my way home, I mulled over how to help out. Calling to mind the young Annie's shooting prowess, I hatched a plan. Mr. Katzenberger at the general store fancied the scheme, agreeing to sell the game I killed to hotels in Cincinnati. My homecoming sweetened with purpose, I set about the business of hunting.

The refined diners in Cincinnati grew partial to my turkeys and pheasants. Instead of hunting with a shotgun like most folks and filling the carcass with bothersome buckshot, I tracked with a rifle. One bullet, removed before the bird hit the table, fashioned meals that were less work and more elegant. As time and practice sharpened my aim, I took part in local shooting matches, managing to store up considerable winnings before the mortified men turned me away. At fifteen, I gathered up all those winnings, paying off the two hundred dollar mortgage on the Shaw farm. I just about burst with joy the day I handed that money to Mother, knowing her home was secure, sweeping away a bit of her worry. Content as a cat stretching in the sun, I spent those years honing my shooting skills and taking pleasure in the family I had missed for so long.

Then came Thanksgiving 1881, a day that tilted my whole world in a brand new direction. Mr. Frost, one of the Cincinnati hotel proprietors who served my fine fowl, caught wind of my being in the city. There for a holiday excursion, I planned to put aside the rifle for a spell, take in the sights, and pay a visit to my sister Lydia. When Mr. Frost proposed a shooting match between his favorite purveyor and a professional sharpshooter passing through town, I said yes.

The fifty dollar purse promised too many farm fixings. Frank Butler was the sharpshooter's name and he boasted all over Cincinnati that he could beat just about anybody. Those gathered that day reckoned to see the backwoods girl defeated. They settled down for the entertaining sight. The most hits out of twenty-five winged targets would grab the purse. Tied at twenty-four perfect shots each, I caught my breath, taking in the thrilling tremble from the crowd. Number twenty-five touched off a commotion to beat the band. Little Annie had won the day. I reeled from my second thunderbolt when Frank Butler's big Irish laugh lifted in delighted merriment. Though publicly defeated by a pint-sized girl ten years younger, he didn't seem embarrassed in the slightest. Shouldering his way through the crowd he walked me to the wagon, flourishing free tickets to his show. Turns out Frank trained dogs about as well as he could shoot. He and his standard poodle, George, made a dazzling team. Frank shot an apple off George's head. George brought me a piece. I gave George a note expressing my deep appreciation. George gave me a box of candy and, well, that's how the courting started. I always gave George his rightful nod for bringing about my marriage to Frank less than a year later.

Cautious as the first spring bud broke through snow, I slowly revealed Frank's story to Mother. Even when seen through the flush of new love, he looked a little rough in certain patches. Born over in Ireland, Frank struck out on his own at thirteen. Sailing across the ocean to America, he traded the work of young muscles for passage. Ever since that time, according to what I could tell, he'd done a little bit of everything. From mucking stalls to a spell as a horse and buggy milkman, Frank had walked a crooked, lively path to his career as sharpshooter and vaudeville entertainer. Along this path, he'd picked up a wife, two children, and a divorce decree. Despite these knockabout circumstances there was a bright core of goodness and humor that shone right through Frank. Why, he even shyly shared his poetry. I had to smile when he made tough little Annie the star of his soft love lyrics. I saw his sparkle right off, and, after mother got to know Frank, she saw it too. She blessed our marriage and ended up loving Frank about as much as I did. As for Frank and me, we partnered for close to fifty years. I never got much past the little bit of education Mrs. Edington gave me and so, didn't get around to reading the great books of the world. But I've heard about some mighty pretty love stories along the way. From what I could tell, none of them measured up to what Frank and I had.

After my wedding, I shook off the Drake County soil and took up the traveling life, helping Frank and his partner set up props for their vaudeville act. Never content to sit still and with my fingers itching to shoot again, I insisted on taking my turn at the targets. From the very first time, the audience loved the wallop of surprise I brought along. Only five feet tall, weighing in at 110 pounds, with the long, loose hair and modest clothes of a young girl, I looked vulnerable. Once the fancy shooting started though, the crowd came to their feet roaring with delight.

Well, it didn't take my shrewd Frank long to see that I offered a more titillating attraction than either him or his partner. Soon, it was little Annie shooting the apples off George's head and smashing tricky targets. With all the new twists and turns in my life, I decided I needed a fresh name as well—Annie Oakley fit me fine and, so, Annie Oakley I became. The pattern for the rest of our stage life gradually took shape. Frank took care of finding work, booking sleeping accommodations and travel, advertising our act, dreaming up new tricks, and caring for the props and guns. I spent my time practicing and, then, practicing some more.

One night in St. Paul, Minnesota it seemed business as usual. The vaudeville theatre bustled with a noisy, excited crowd. Unknown to me, square in the middle of it all with an inscrutable face and crossed arms, sat the Sioux chief, Sitting Bull. Moving around the white man's world to satisfy his curiosity about such mystifying ways, the chief happened to be on a tour of the city. After my act, he insisted on meeting me. He felt the presence of the Great Spirit in my gifts and the presence of his long dead daughter in my small, athletic form and dark hair. Then and there he adopted me as his own, showering me with gifts. My favorite treasure became a pair of battered moccasins, handmade by his daughter and worn at the Battle of Little Big Horn. He gifted me with a new name, too, "Little Sure Shot." Frank, always quick to see an advertising opportunity, made use of that name and my status as Sitting Bull's adopted daughter for the rest of my career. Later, Sitting Bull and I ended up touring together with Buffalo Bill's Wild West Show. Our bond ran deep, lasting until his death in 1890.

Soon after my meeting with Sitting Bull, Frank and I joined the Sells Brothers' Circus. The uncertainty of the vaudeville life just wore Frank and me down. We soon figured out that we had jumped from the nettles into the briar patch. The Sells Brothers, it turned out, ran a careless outfit. Offended by the shoddy, dangerous equipment and poor provisions for both people and animals, we began to look around again.

Then, as sometimes happens, fate intervened. While in New Orleans performing with the circus, Frank and I heard stories about Buffalo Bill's Wild West Show across town. We headed that way. Our practiced eyes quickly took in the organized and humane operation. The only problem being they already had a world champion sharpshooter. We got turned down flat when we tried to hire on. Not long after, rumor had it that the aging marksman had quit. Frank and I once again put ourselves square in Buffalo Bill's sights. With his comely, bearded face crinkling in amusement, the flamboyant showman took in my petite frame and girlish appearance, laughingly skeptical that I could even lift the burly sharpshooter's abandoned guns. My silver-tongued Frank persuaded him to give me a try anyway.

The audition day finally arrived. Frank and I showed up early so I could practice while the Wild West family pranced and marched in the big parade. We both noticed a lone figure loitering close by but figured him to be a curious onlooker. After my practice, the dapper man ran toward us, holding onto his derby hat and waving a cane in excitement. Nate Salsbury, Buffalo Bill's business partner, had just witnessed his show's star act for the next seventeen years. He hired me on the spot.

From that moment on, my life took on a dizzying intensity. Folks everywhere flocked to Buffalo Bill's spectacular pageantry. Almost everyone knew of some adventurous soul who had struck out for the West. Buffalo Bill intended to feed the hungry curiosity of those who stayed behind. With a cast including hundreds of people and animals, props so big they had to be taken apart when moved, and Buffalo Bill's theatrical flair, the Wild West came alive, just as advertised. Having experienced the rough glory of it all himself as a scout, Pony Express rider, hunter, and soldier, the long-haired Colonel brought authenticity to the thrilling scenes. Stagecoach robberies, Indian attacks, burning cabins, battle scenes, and amazing acts of roping, shooting, and horseback riding opened up the world of bold adventure, even to those who never left home.

Leading the show as one of the first acts, I played on my dainty demeanor by skipping childishly into the arena. Blowing airy kisses, I duplicated the ruse of my vaudeville days. Before the crowd knew what hit them, the Colonel's "Little Missy" became a trick-shooting, swift-riding cowgirl. Throughout those years, Frank devised all manner of amazing feats for me to perform. Up to sixty glass balls in a row shattered by my bullseye accuracy released drifting feathers in the air. Using a mirror and, at times, even a knife blade, I hit the marks behind me with rapid precision. Lying on the ground or draped across chairs, I shot targets with the same ease and accuracy as I did standing up. I tossed balls in the air, circled prettily around, and then shattered them to pieces. From ninety feet, I shot playing cards turned sideways and, before they hit the ground, pounded more holes into them. Also at ninety feet, I could nail an airborne dime. From the back of a galloping horse, I hit each target Frank released, firing from every angle—astride, side-saddle, and even standing up. The tricks, limited only by Frank's imagination, grew more daring and unbelievable as the years passed. Headlines touted my dazzling skill and crowds left the show grounds doubting their own eyes.

Buffalo Bill's Wild West Show grew in majesty and acclaim. We crossed the ocean to perform for Queen Victoria's Golden Jubilee in 1887. Crowned heads throughout Europe gathered to watch the blazing tales of the American West. I quickly grabbed star billing and was often invited to perform in private audiences and exclusive gun clubs. I walked the halls of palaces, broke bread with world leaders, and collected medals and costly gifts in every country we toured. Queen Victoria herself held my hand and called me a clever little girl. European fashion designers copied the flair and sass of my homemade costumes. Flabbergasted by the elevated outcome of her sewing lessons, Mrs. Edington shook her head over the exploits of plain little Annie.

In 1889 we headed back to Europe for the World's Fair in Paris. Celebrating the hundred-year anniversary of the French Revolution, crowds gazed in awe at the magnificent Eiffel tower built specially for the exposition. Still reeling from that remarkable sight, they gawked at the diminutive cowgirl who bested their champion marksmen. Everyone from shoeshine boys on the corner to elegantly attired blue bloods recognized the American sharpshooter.

The Chicago's World Fair, built to celebrate the four hundredth anniversary of Columbus' New World discovery, opened in the summer of 1893. Declaring the Wild West Show far too unruly for the sophisticated White City constructed for the occasion, the fair officials denied us space. Not one to accept defeat, Buffalo Bill opened his show just a puddle jump from the fair's front gates. Breaking records, we performed for about 6,000,000 onlookers that summer. It turned out that no trip to the World's Fair rounded out without a stop at the Wild West Show across the way.

During leisure times, the Wild West family strolled along the boulevards of the White City, our unruly western chatter finding an easy rhythm with the thrum of excitement. The Ferris Wheel, a twirling circle invented to outdo the Eiffel Tower from the previous World's Fair, lifted us high above where we walked. The nighttime rides on the big wheel were the ones we could not get enough of. That's when those new electric lights switched on, spreading across the fair's six hundred acres, brighter even than the stars above. Swaying two hundred feet in the air, I thought about how far a body can come in one lifetime.

And then there were, of course, the shows in all the towns and cities with a yen for thrills.

Eventually becoming one of the most recognized women in America, I earned, at my zenith, as much money as the President of the United States. But through all the noise and glitter I kept my feet firmly planted on the ground. I always honored my Quaker modesty. Stung early by poverty, Frank and I both held on to frugal habits. Battling the chaos of constant travel with what some family members called obsessive behavior, I followed an unwavering discipline of healthy food, good sleep, and unflagging practice.

Mine and Frank's large tent became the quiet heart of the Wild West Show. Children, cowboys, and Indian braves gathered like chickens to a roost, finding rest in our homey spot. Decorated with photographs, sentimental keepsakes, inviting furniture, satin pillows, rugs, and curtains, our tent embraced them all. Those who stepped across our welcome mat most likely found Frank reading or writing and me sewing or embroidering. We managed to make a home wherever we went.

Fastidious with my body as well as my surroundings, I bathed each morning in a collapsible bathtub and ended each day with a witch hazel rub. Jars of creams and hair tonics helped maintain my youthful appearance. I guess you might say little Annie flirted with vanity.

One dark night in 1901 the fast-moving Wild West train slammed head on into an oncoming locomotive. Frank wasn't hurt. Thrown from my bed, I damaged my spine. After several surgeries we decided it was time to pull back from the hectic demands of Buffalo Bill's traveling show.

In our retirement, Frank and I, blessed by excess and already inclined to generosity, threw ourselves into charity work. Passionate about improving the lives of women, I gave free shooting lessons to willing ladies all over the country. Believing that women should be able to handle guns as easily as they handled babies, I encouraged them to develop habits of independence and outdoor exercise, as well as to fearlessly defend themselves. Personally bereaved by the tragedy of tuberculosis through the death of two sisters, I melted down my medals and donated the proceeds to sanatoriums. Never forgetting the sad stories housed in the Drake County Infirmary, I quietly paid for the education of twenty girls, each one an orphan. At the outbreak of both the Spanish American War and World War I, I wrote letters to the presidents, offering to lead troops of female soldiers. Neither McKinley nor Roosevelt took me up on the idea, so I settled for raising money. Frank and I trained our good pal Dave, an English Setter, to sniff out coins and bills wrapped in handkerchiefs. Every penny Dave ferreted out went to the Red Cross. Called the "Red Cross Dog," Dave collected thousands of dollars. He became quite famous in his own right, proudly posing for pictures, but leaving the interviews to his more talkative associates.

I often said about Frank and myself, that we worked as hard as little hound pups at a rabbit hole. At the end, we just wore out. After a car accident, I never really had the strength to get much better. Then Dave got hit by a car and died. His loss sapped me dry. When I finally left this world, Frank, already sick himself, just quit eating and followed along behind me eighteen days later.

Some speculate that the pesky lead from the ammunition I handled all those years poisoned my blood. I don't speculate. I figure that how you finally ride away shrinks small next to how you pass through your days. Where I passed, I aimed high.

DON CADDEN

Cow Women

Those cowgirls you see in the magazines
They all look pretty and slick
Not a hair out of place, face made up
Lots of sexy pink lipstick

The high-dollar jeans look painted on
To a body with a tight behind
Man-made boobs peek out of rhinestone shirts
That'll blow a cowboy's mind

Now the women I work with don't dress like that
But they've all got plenty of sand
These ol' gals are cowboys to the bone
They'll dang sure make you a hand

They can drag a calf on a half-broke horse
Or be part of the flankin' crew
They'll take a knife, change a bull to a steer
Then make you some oyster stew

I've seen 'em covered with guacamole
When preg checking time comes around
Then wash up clean in a water trough
And head for the big dance in town

They'll take the outside circle
Busting the brush in a lope
Then put some snot-slingin' cow in the pen
Before you can shake out your rope

If you think "cowboy" is a term of gender
You've been watching too much TV
I've seen women make the kind of hand
Most men just try to be

When those city gals marched for women's lib
They should have come out West
They could have learned equality
In muck boots and a Carhartt vest

Our girls look good in their worn-out jeans
Packin' a fifty-pound bag of cake
Or taking a pistol or long-handled hoe
To a pissed-off rattlesnake

So keep your fancy magazines
And the models who set all the trends
Give me a gal with some poop on her boots
And lots of bottom end

DAVID LAVAR COY

The Navajo Woman

Proud of her Indian heritage,
Eleanor, half Apache,
shows her co-workers at Wal-Mart
a newspaper photo of a Navajo woman
who at a hundred looks younger,

who still cooks on a wood-burning stove,
herds her flock of sheep with a willow switch,
even chops her own wood, who dresses
in wool dyed by hand, wears bracelets
made of turquoise, earrings carved from bone,

whose eyes shine, showing
she still loves life. Two of Eleanor's co-workers,
women in their forties, complain
they will never see sixty, and stuff themselves
with hotdogs and milkshakes,

They recognize that age worn well
is a dignity they'll never realize.
The Navajo woman credits her long life
to hard work, self-discipline, and luck,
says Death has not noticed her yet.

She is expecting him, has been waiting
a long time, has hung a red buffalo skull
over her front door to catch his attention.

Changing Woman

Clouds tear apart and reform above the harsh landscape. Snowfall comes sparse, rushes into fullness, north-wind flakes fast blown to sixteen compass points. Late afternoon, one day into a new year and I'm headed south, halfway between Page and Cameron. The engine sounds happy and the heater's still not working. Arizona winter cuts through the cab of the truck, dry snow blows across the asphalt. Almost no traffic.

I'm wearing my interview outfit—full skirt and velveteen blouse, grandmother's silver concho belt, and my own mother's turquoise necklace. My single long braid unraveled, it tangles in the Pendleton blanket around my shoulders. My healed finger throbs where I tore the nail during a dig in Utah in August.

Six cars and four pickup trucks in the trading post parking lot—Edward's truck is hooked to a horse trailer filled with lumber, fence posts, rolls of baling wire, a couple of old doors.

The cash register girl is wearing a Flagstaff Eagles jersey over a wool sweater. Two boys flirt with her: long hair, baseball caps, and heavy metal t-shirts.

"Restaurant's still open?" I say.

"Yes, ma'am," says the girl. They all lower their eyes, respectfully, to me, their elder; and the cold weather I've been ignoring makes itself known in my thirty-five-year-old bones and joints.

"I went to high school in Monument Valley," I say. "The Mustangs. I played on the basketball team. My people are from around there. I'm Ruth Yazzie, Bit'ahnii, born for Táchii'nii. My mother's father is Tódích'íi'nii and my father's father is Ta'neeszahnii." And even though I can see her in the back of the trading post, I ask politely, "Is Betsy here today?"

"She's here now. She likes it when there're no visitors—"

I wind my way through bottled water, soda pop, cigarettes, and potato chips; bins of polished rocks, thin t-shirts, cheap leather moccasins, toy spears with rubber points. Betsy's hands move along the weave with slow assurance: heald, warp thread, batten, comb—rhythmic fingers building up a complex Storm Pattern. She's about three-quarters of the way finished; cream, tan, grey, and black. Not my biological grandmother, but so much a part of my life that it would be rude not to call her that.

I stand and wait.

Two minutes pass.

Betsy waves to me to sit down.

"Good afternoon, Grandmother."

"Ya'at'eeh, child," she says.

"It's coming along. The colors of the earth—what could be more beautiful?"

"I think this is one of the last ones. My eyes—each year it gets harder to see. And my arthritis—it never gets better. The medicine helps, but—" she purses her lips to point to the girl at the cash register. "My grand-niece, Angela. She's learning—when she's not chasing boys. She will carry on where I leave off. One day, it will be that girl sitting here, putting on a show for the summer tourists."

"You put in the spirit line already," I say.

"Pah! A woman your age, showing off your knowledge!"

"Please, tell me the story again?"

"Always wanting to hear the stories—over and over."

"I'm a cultural anthropologist. It's my job."

"In the Third World, Spider Woman received her instructions. The holy people told her to weave a pattern in the Third World. 'What is that?' she said. She didn't know what weaving was or how to do it. One day the thread came out of her hand and she started making twisty patterns. Not a weaving, just winding the thread this way and that. Once she could see the thread moving, she understood what that meant, what weaving meant. Spider Man built the loom for her—oh yes, they argued about what the posts and crossbeams meant! The symbols—they argued about what everything represented. Sky and earth, sunbeams, crystals, and lightning. The batten was white shell—but mine is made of wood! The spindles were lightning and rain—coal, turquoise, abalone, and white shell.

"They argued about what to call the things that he made for her. But when it was made, she was the only one who would use it. Now, we don't argue. The men know how to build the loom, and of course they help with the sheep, sometimes with gathering bark and roots and what-you-will for dying the wool. The women do the spinning. We do the carding. The spirit line lets my spirit escape from the pattern—the pattern is in my mind, and I don't want my mind trapped in this pattern. Since Spider Woman is always with me, I don't want her to be trapped in the pattern either. Then, I might never weave a good rug again.

"Spider Woman gave the Hero Twins directions. Naayéé' Neizghání, Monster Slayer, and Tóbájíshchíní, Child of the Water—she told them how to find their father, Jóhonaa'éí, The Sun, The One Who Rules the Day. That's part of the story, but I think today you need to hear something else. You look like sadness. I'll skip that part about their father, I know you know it.

"After the Twins met their father, they went to kill the monsters that were killing the Diné. They killed the monsters and they brought back the scalps and body parts. They hung these outside their mother Changing Woman's home. What I want to tell you today is this: Every time Changing Woman even looked at those tokens of the monsters, she had to cleanse herself with pollen and chanting."

"I never heard that part before," I say.

"What would you do if you had those leftover things hanging outside your home? Every time you walked past, every time you saw those bad things, you would want to cleanse yourself." She slips a shuttle through the warp. "But you know this story—and you tell it yourself, I'm sure, when you teach your students at the university. I still don't understand how someone can make a living by writing down all these stories."

"Sometimes I tell this story," I say. "But I like the way you tell it. And it's never the same—it's always a little different. I never heard that part about Changing Woman cleaning herself when she looked at the things the Twins brought her. Every time you tell a story, I learn more. I listen, so I can make a written record. Not so many young people know or tell the stories anymore."

"You make books—who reads the books? Diné? Or bilagáana?"

"A little of both," I say.

"Still have the weaving I gave you?"

"Of course!" I say, even though I hate to tell lies. "Do you have a ride home tonight?"

"Your friend Edward said he would take me home," she says. "I trust him—he knows every dirt road in four states. Go talk to him. His son is sick again."

"Thank you. I'll see you again before I leave."

Edward's sitting alone in the restaurant. Jeans and a long-sleeved t-shirt, hooded sweatshirt, denim jacket, worn boots. Hair long and knotted in the back the old way, tsiiyééł, something I never learned to do for myself. Topographic map spread out on the table.

"Ya'at'eeh, Professor Yazzie." Edward leans over, offers me part of a chocolate bar.

"Coffee and candy on a cold afternoon," I say. "Ya'at'eeh, Mr. Edward Begay."

"Mister?" He laughs.

"Professor?" I laugh, too.

The server is another quiet teenage girl. She refrains from making eye contact, stares respectfully just past my shoulder, fills my cup.

"Vegetarian fry bread taco to go," I say. "And french fries and coffee. And one slice of apple pie."

"That's healthy," says Edward.

"Almost as good as heating up a can of beans on an open fire."

"Best beans I've ever had."

"Me, too."

"People say we make a weird couple," he says. "Hiking into the empty canyons for days at a time."

"That's where the artifacts are," I say. "More grave robbers on our lands every day. We're saving the past. And you know the land better than anyone else—like it's a part of your own self. What do people say?"

"Just gossip . . . because we've know each other for years now."

I touch his hand—a habit I've picked up from working around white people at the university. He radiates strength and sadness. "I'm glad we're friends. It's Andrew, isn't it?"

"Saw him at Christmas. Drove over to Crown Point for a few days. Some of his mom's clan are just north of there. He was sick though the whole time. Leukemia, you know? They did a sing for him, but it didn't help. It's the stuff that's leaked into the wells, into the water. It's the poison wind blowing off the mine tailings. If I'd known, things would be different. The council can't help, and the government is always investigating and reviewing everything. They won't take responsibility for the private mining companies coming in and ruining the land."

"Whatever you need," I say, "whatever I can do for you—you let me know. We're like brother and sister."

"I'll remember that. You're wearing your interview outfit."

"It puts the elders at ease—good intentions don't always show through."

"My older sister dresses like that all the time. She was Miss Navajo Nation one year back in the nineties. Never got over it."

"Grand Canyon?" I trace the Little Colorado with my finger. Pencil markings. "What is there left to recover in a National Park?"

"Well," he says, "Tatahatso Point is on Reservation land, but drop down into Tatahatso Canyon—part of the Park—there's plenty to see and record and retrieve, if you want to. This time I have permission. Filed for a permit and got it. Not like that time in New Mexico."

"When do we leave?" I say.

"I've already been down there twice. It's an untouched cliff dwelling, high above the river and set well back. Climbing steps carved into the rock centuries ago, but you have to know where to look. Pottery, fabric remnants, tools—and this."

I open the envelope above the map. A tiny copper bell; round and oxidized green.

"Even I know what that means," says Edward. "It was buried beneath a hearth. I documented what I did—took photos and made a short video with my phone."

"Grand Canyon cliff dwellers trading with a culture in what is now Northern Mexico," I say. "This one thing could completely change current theories on cultural dispersion."

"I'm thinking spring, after the last thaw. There's no trail so the footing is iffy and we'll be in canyon shade most of the time. Early March?"

"It's a date."

The girl brings my food in a folded paper box.

"In February I'll be in Gallup and Crown Point," I say. "I would like to stop in and see your son. Would his mother's family allow that?"

"Shouldn't be a problem, but I'll let them know. Headed home?"

"I've been gone six days."

"Hardly worth paying rent on that little house."

"Springtime," I say. "Last thaw. We'll get together then."

"How will I find you?" he says.

"I'll find you. So long. Hágoónee'."

"Hágoónee', Ruth."

Back in the trading post Besty's packing up her yarns and tools.

"You and Edward had a nice talk?" she says.

"We're just good friends," I say. "Everyone knows that."

"Some of the best marriages start with friendship—trust and respect."

"Grandmother, I have to go now."

"Yes, yes; always travelling and listening to stories. I guess I'll see you when I see you."

"Always," I say.

*

Sleepiness makes itself known. Flagstaff can wait another day. I stop at the Anasazi Inn, ten miles south of the trading post. The sheets are clean and the wall heater works; the toilet tank drains and re-fills, and a disinfectant perfume lingers in the air. Only two other vehicles are in the parking lot, though there's a background hum of occasional trucks and cars on 89A. A framed poster of an idyllic tropical paradise, completely out of place.

What we are when we are alone.

A memory.

Wendy and I meeting for the first time at a faculty mixer at the university. She takes me to her studio at midnight, shows me her paintings; we talk art and stories, drink tea until dawn when sunrise ignites something between us. Light as feathers, we phone the university, cancel our classes for the day, linger together without a knowledge of time. How I yielded to her, and kept yielding for two years.

I look at my phone, tempted, but there's no signal. Stretch my legs and wriggle my rear end in the chair. Stare at cold bread and congealed grease in the takeout box.

This hunger.

*

The next morning I'm holding a supermarket bouquet outside Wendy's condo on the east side of Flagstaff. A scattering of pine needles on the welcome mat from a dried-out wreath. Five suitcases, rolls of paper and canvas, a stack of boxes just inside the door. She takes the flowers in silence, with a look I can't interpret.

"Leaving tomorrow," says Wendy. "I'll be in New Mexico for at least a month, maybe longer. I worked out this arrangement with the university. I'm still an associate professor, but I'm not teaching this year or doing any tutorials."

"Your hair—" I say.

"Things change. Short and red instead of long and blonde."

"What's in New Mexico?"

"A studio in Santa Fe with a bathroom and a kitchen that I can barely afford, but that's where the money is."

I point to the Storm Pattern weaving on the wall. "I saw the woman who wove that, just yesterday."

"I put it there to remind me of you."

She arranges the flowers in a vase. Crosses the room, pulls me into an embrace. One of us clings. Sleet prickles the roof; a battery clock clicks in another room. Which clock? Which room? I want to enter that room, tomorrow's room, where clocks tick yet time stands still.

A large plush teddy bear against the pillows, wearing an NAU t-shirt.

"Who's that?"

"Miss Bear. She keeps me company at night."

"You're kidding."

"I'm not embarrassed if that's what you mean."

I peel off all my clothing. Naked, I know my power.

"I could swallow you completely right now," I say.

"You feel the same," says Wendy. "I remember everything."

"That means we're still connected."

"We should stop talking now."

*

Gray light comes from a single window. Heavy snow obscures the world.

"Do you remember why you left?" I say.

"Yes," says Wendy. "Do you?"

"Careers, opportunities—commitments—I had no idea you were leaving again tomorrow."

"Santa Fe is a big thing for me. This is it. This is me finally making it in the real art world."

"You left me to be a professional artist?"

"I was already a professional artist. You're a professional anthropologist. You've published three books. People come to you for advice and information because you're the best in your field. I want to be the best, too. I want to get paid for being the best. There's nothing wrong with that."

"I feel like two years are erased from my life," I say.

"You spent so many days on the road, all the interviews. In the beginning we were together all the time. Then, it wasn't like that anymore."

"I live through my work."

"That's what I'm doing," she says. "I'm living my life through my artwork." She slides down next to me on the bed.

"I think I'm still in love with you," I say. "Tomorrow—"

"Be here now," she says.

And I yield.

*

It's night when I get home. I use my foot to clear snow from the front steps. Little drifts of powder on the screened-in porch. Junk mail, silence, cold. Dry, but not musty. I run two loads of laundry and microwave dinner. Shower, check my phone messages, and answer emails from students registered for my spring classes. Pillows propped against the headboard, I try to read a mystery thriller I started in November; but it pales against my movement through arid landscapes. I turn off the light and listen to the faint voices of a house in winter.

*

Mondays hold promise until mid-morning.

The top sheet in the plastic box on the door is a note about parking permits for lots F-1 and F-3. My office smells syrupy-sweet from three-week-old flowers on my desk. A parting gift from Ewa, already returned to the Cracow University of Economics—and a husband and two children, if that were true. I half hoped that being with her would help me forget the past.

Dust covers books, pottery, tools, and maps. I set the vase and dead blossoms in the wastebasket outside my door.

"Good morning? Dr. Yazzie?" The department secretary stops and smiles. "I didn't know you were back. I'm reminding everyone about the meeting."

"Kirsten. Hello. The meeting?"

"The budget committee is giving another presentation and participation is mandatory."

"Restrictions on off-campus activities," I say. "Archaeology, anthropology, and geology; studies where the learning takes place in the field. All of the money directed into the Hospitality, Education, and Forestry programs. This is not why I became a teacher."

"And I heard from my friend Sheila over in the registrar's office that we can expect another pitch for web-based learning and on-line diplomas. I know how much you hate that." She spins on high heels and clicks down the hall to spread the bad news.

I flip a calendar page, cross out days gone by. Spring semester starts January twelfth; today is the third. Outside, clouds pour over the San Francisco Peaks, west to east.

Kirsten passes the door again.

"Starts at nine-thirty. The big meeting room on the first floor."

A clear circle on my desk where a vase of flowers rested.

I pick up my bag, lock the door, and leave the building.

*

Holiday priced frozen hams and turkeys. I drop four of each in the cart. Canned tomatoes and beans, bags of rice, flour, and sugar. Fruit, vegetables, twelve packs of soda pop, bags of candy, cartons of cigarettes. Cardboard boxes from the back of the store. Pack it all in the bed of the truck with a box of books for my uncle, and cover it with a plastic tarp. Slip off my watch and turn off my phone.

Three hours of driving east to Chambers where I fill up the tank, head north on 191. Halfway to Ganado, I pull off at a place where jewelry and pottery roadside booths stand empty, sun-bleached red paint over gray plywood. Stretch my legs and breathe the tang of wet piñon and juniper. The soft, undulating landscape reminds me of Wendy's Georgia O'Keeffe-inspired paintings. I daydream a jumble of images: art studios, dusty archaeological digs, a gay bar in Phoenix. Horses, hospitals, mother. Low clouds drift past; minutes pass before I realize I'm being watched.

A slight movement in the trees. I take a step and a pair of yellow eyes flicker, blink, move toward me. I move with purpose to the edge of the trees; coyote slinks into invisibility.

A raven caws once and flies away.

*

Half an hour later I park in front of my Aunt Mary and Uncle Albert's house in Chinle. Two dogs run in delirious circles. My aunt stirs mutton stew on the stove top, stacks fresh fry bread on the counter. We sit down to dinner.

"You like that, Ruthie?" says my aunt. "Take some with you when you leave. So thin! You need to take care of yourself."

"When you buy food in a box at a grocery store, you get a lot of air," says my uncle. "And the food tastes like the box."

"I'm so busy right now," I say. "I'm teaching three classes this semester and I've agreed to a couple of graduate student tutorials."

"Did you finish your new book?" says my aunt.

"Not yet. That's one of the reasons I'm here. I scheduled an interview with two elders at the senior center in Round Rock. From there I'll go on to Mexican Water, Tes Nez Iah, Dennehotso, Kayenta, Tsegi, and Tonalea."

"Ah! Never in one place. Stay and visit. I'll call your sister and she can bring her kids. When was the last time you saw your nephews? You know how fast they grow. I'll call Agnes now."

"Auntie," I say, "Gallup is a two hour drive—besides, they were here at Christmas."

"What about your father? Do you have time for him?"

"Tomorrow morning I'll go to the interview in Round Rock. Then I'll just go on to Mexican Water."

"You and your sister and us two old farts are all he's got left. Albert goes over about once a month or so and stays a few days. Your sister goes up two, three times a year. Takes the kids and her husband, too."

Against my aunt's protests I help wash the dishes. Bring my uncle his cigarettes, lighter, and one of the paperback novels. After that I sit on a back step outside, wrapped in my parka and blanket, face a scattering of car parts and plastic toys. The dogs settle at my feet. Half an hour later my uncle joins me. He lights and puffs his cigarette.

"I don't know if you remember," he says, "but the winters around here used to be really bad. Freezing cold even during the day. We had more snow, too. 'Course that was when we lived in the canyon and we had to keep the fire going day and night to keep warm."

"I was happy," I say. "I had everything I wanted."

"That's because you didn't want much. Your mother would have been proud of you. Going to college back east and becoming a teacher right here at the University. And always coming home with food and gifts."

"It's the right thing to do. It's the way we live."

"Not too many young people think that way now."

"I'm not that young anymore, uncle."

"James lives like that. He has that wood-burning stove from the old place. Of course now he has some local kids cut and haul the wood for him. Pays them out of what you and your sister send him every month. That's also the right thing to do—caring for one's parents." I hear the pride in his voice. "Your friend didn't come with you?"

For the second time in three days I tell a lie. "Wendy's really busy with a one-woman show at a gallery in Santa Fe. It's a very prestigious place and she wanted to be there to oversee everything. All of the paintings have to be photographed for a catalogue."

"Any new stories to share?"

"I saw Betsy Manygoats a few days ago in Cameron. She told me part of the Spider Woman story again and something new about Changing Woman. And—" and I hesitate—"I have a story of my own. A coyote story." I tell him about my encounter.

"Maybe it was a dog," he says. "Wild dog packs all around the towns. They wait at the groceries and markets for handouts."

"It was a coyote, all right."

"Maybe it was nothing. Sometimes a coyote is just a coyote. But, you know, if I were you I wouldn't tell anyone else just yet. Maybe you could mention it to those elders up at Round Rock."

Inside we pour cups of coffee and join my aunt at the cleared kitchen table.

"Father did pretty well with Agnes and me those first years when he was alone," I say. "Even when I was a kid I could see he was sad. We knew that. Agnes and I will always be grateful that you took us in."

"When will you settle down?" says my uncle. "Your little sister—already married and two kids—"

"Settle down?" I say. "Like my sister? We couldn't be more different."

"No, not much chance of that," says my aunt. "Agnes was only five years old when you came to live with us. She takes after me, but you—ah, Ruthie. You are your mother's daughter."

*

A blue pickup truck with a gray fender parked next to the Round Rock Chapter House, in the sun and out of the wind. A girl sees me and waves a set of keys.

"Emma Tsedah," she says. "I live over in Lukachukai. I agreed to drive over here—that's my truck. The man with the red shirt is Nelson Tso, my great-uncle on my mother's mother's side. The other guy is his friend, Wayne Huerta. I'll do the formal introductions inside, is that okay?"

Emma makes coffee in the kitchen, opens a package of doughnuts. I give the three-minute version of who I am, what I do, and why I'm there. Place the digital recorder on the tabletop, explain how I'll record their stories and our conversation.

"What do you want us to talk about?" says Nelson.

"Everything and anything," I say. "I like the stories we all share; but I like hearing the stories of each person's life, too. History books only tell us part of who we are."

"After Vietnam, I worked as a cook in Farmington for years," says Nelson. "I wanted to be a silversmith like my grandfather. I worked with silver whenever I could, but never got real good at it."

"When we were teenagers we rode every rodeo we could," says Wayne. "I can tell you about that."

"I'll listen," I say.

Three hours: memories of life among the People as far back as the 1950s: healing ceremonies, sheep herding, girlfriends, motorcycles, horses, war, and always families.

"Except for your military service, you always lived and worked on the Res?" I say.

"We both worked in the mines for a couple years," says Nelson. "That's why I have this cough—all the dust. Right away I could see it was a bad place. Church Rock, before that big tailings spill in the Puerco River. That was wrong."

"What they did," says Wayne, "is take the ore from the ground and leave behind a mess—a big wound in the earth. We were lucky—some worked there for years and got sick from cancer and some died because of the poison in the river." At noon Emma takes a casserole from the oven, makes more coffee.

"I have a story," she says. "It's okay to tell shapechanger stories in the winter, right?"

"Yes," I say. I plug in the charger cord for the recorder.

"One night, it was summer and I was thirteen and some of us were bored and hanging out around the middle school right here in Round Rock. There's not much for kids to do in the summer around here. It was right after sunset, you know, when there's barely enough light to see, just before it gets dark. There were five of us and Benny Allen had some cigarettes he'd swiped from his dad and a twelve pack his older brother got for us and we were just hanging out. It was the first time I smoked a cigarette or drank a beer. We were being kids, you know, just talking and telling jokes when Benny says, real quiet, 'Look.' And we look over where the trees are and there's two coyotes watching us. Just standing there. And you know those old stories—about the witches spying on people and looking for places to cause trouble—I can tell you they're true."

The men are silent, personal stories forgotten for the moment.

"I've heard witches can travel great distances," I say. "Have you heard that?"

"They can fly around the Earth in one night," says Wayne. "Always looking for trouble. Always listening to see if people are talking about them. Coyote is only one of their disguises. Mostly they look like regular people."

"Those coyotes stared at us like they were thinking things through," says Emma.

"Maybe they were following you?" I say.

"Yeah, like they were waiting to see what we would do next."

"Then what happened?"

"That night was fun but kind of weird. After a few minutes the coyotes just slipped away. Or maybe they were hiding in the shadows and still watching, but I didn't feel that at the time. Hanging out with my friends and then those coyotes. I threw up and that was the first and last time I drank alcohol. After that I found out how easy it is to bootleg beer and liquor on the Res. My friend Annie wasn't so lucky. She lives in Albuquerque and hangs out in bars all the time. It's really bad what she has to do to get by. Alcoholism and bootlegging are big problems around here. Worse than the lack of jobs."

"I saw a coyote yesterday," I say. "Watching me." I tell my own brief story.

"That's like what happened to me," says Emma. "My father says when there're two people together there can be peace or trouble. But one person and a shapechanger always leads to trouble. So we have to be careful of what we say and do."

"Naayéé' Neizghání left many monsters alive at the beginning," says Nelson. He nods to Emma. "His mother, Asdzą́ą́ Nádleehé, told him to let them live.

Old age, hunger, cold, and being poor—those things are still with us. Those things come to us in many forms."

"I know that story," says Emma. "But the way I heard it, Changing Woman tells Monster Slayer where the last monsters are—the ones we still have. The monsters explain why they are needed in the world and Monster Slayer spares them."

"She wanted to keep everything evened out," I say. "Not too much good, not too much bad. Hózhó. Balance. So now we have alcoholism, uranium mines and cancer, an indifferent federal government. Unbelievable poverty. People who take and use others for their own ends."

Emma clears away our plates and cups.

"Tell her about the time at the rodeo in Window Rock when that man's horse threw him and ran off with the boots still in the stirrups," says Nelson.

Wayne obliges and his friend faithfully corrects him.

We finish mid-afternoon. Emma locks the door and I place a cardboard box in the back of her truck.

The men dig through the box. Two canned hams, salt, sugar, sacks of flour and pinto beans, a mesh bag of oranges. Sports magazines, tobacco, and candy. They acknowledge the gifts with smiles.

Emma walks me back to my own truck.

"I'm taking classes at the NAU extension sites in Chinle and Kayenta," she says. "I want to enroll at NAU or U of A next year. I'd like to be a counselor or a psychologist and come back here and work in all of these little towns. We really need someone like that around here. You think I can do it?"

"You're doing it now," I say. "Just a few more years to gather the book learning. You've got a good heart. That's what's important. Stay true to your heart."

Driving north to Mexican Water I remember Wendy wanting to be paid for "being the best." Imagine the balance between good and bad, right and wrong.

*

I wait in the truck for two, five, eight minutes. My father's house is cinderblock and pre-fabricated panels, one of a scattering of similar houses. A trickle of chimney smoke. An old truck, a curious blue horse in the corral.

Baggy jeans, an orange sweatshirt, a Phoenix Suns baseball cap. Slower than I remember. I bring in a box of food. The kitchen is spotless and warmth fills the air. Tea towels and a pleated valence above the sink. Hand lotion on the window sill.

"You hungry or checking up on me?" he says.

"I'm—it looks like your kitchen—like a woman—"

He grins. "I'm not old yet."

"Do I know her?"

"Louise," he says. "She lives over in Teec Nos Pos with her son and daughter. You don't know her. Dinner is a casserole and baked potatoes. Albert called—we knew you were coming. Louise wanted to make something nice for you—she said now was not the right time for you to meet though. It's good that you think of me. I'm where I should be. I like living here—I can ride out into the canyons anytime. I know pretty much everyone in this area. It's a good place. What about you, Ruthie? Are you where you belong?"

"It's so cold!" I say. I feel the top of the old wood-burning stove; add newspaper and kindling, strike a match.

"You don't need to do that," says my father.

"I'm doing it for me. The heater in my truck doesn't work. Is the propane still hooked up for the stove? Uncle Albert says some boys cut your wood for you."

"They take the water tank to get filled, too."

I stare hard at the blossoming fire.

"Everything is good," he says. "I just miss my daughters and grandchildren. I go over to the senior center. The ladies bring some nice dishes. We have bingo and card games."

"You know Wayne Huerta and Nelson Tso? I interviewed them today."

"Those two bullshitters? You didn't pay them, did you? They'll talk your ear off. I don't think I've ever heard either one of them tell the truth."

"I've got my ways," I say. "They told me some stuff that was new and true."

He sits in a cushioned recliner, a gift from Agnes and her husband. A neatly-stitched tear along one arm of a sagging sofa.

"Do you need me, Daddy?"

"I just need you to be my daughter."

"I'm not a little kid anymore—"

"Forget it," he says. "You spend the night—one night—then go on again. I know better than to tell you to stand still."

After dinner we bring water to the horse, stand awhile in almost-darkness. Stars appear, the Milky Way is close and bright.

"Like when we lived in the canyon," says my father.

"Uncle and I were talking about that. Was it really colder then?"

"Eh. The older one gets, the colder one gets."

"You said everything is good," I say. "Are you happy?"

"As much as anyone can be."

The last strip of light fades on the horizon, and I know we're both thinking about the same person.

*

Six days later I'm driving south again to Cameron from Tuba City. The sky is low and gray. I've changed into jeans and a sweater. Six days of interviews; I've stayed with families in their homes, motels on 160 twice. Dozens of hours of stories recorded and saved. I wonder about typing transcripts; I wonder about two graduate student tutorials. Three classes, emails, syllabi, meetings. A dust-covered desk surrounded by books that only people like me read. Dead flowers.

Four cars and two semis in the parking lot. Inside, the trading post is almost empty. Betsy's loom is covered with a bed sheet; in the restaurant the truck drivers check their phones and sip coffee. A young couple with a baby, a table circled with retirees. I leave without ordering anything to go.

Snowfall, night. A memory.

*

I'm five years old, balanced on the top rail of the fence around the corral, whispering for the red mare to come closer until I can grab her mane and pull myself onto her back. Wet snow melts in my hair and there's a sudden awareness that I have wings and will always be able to fly. Circling the corral—a single crack of winter lightning—and the mare tosses me. I scream; Mother

50

and Aunt Mary rush outside from the warmth of winter stories, slip between the rails. Auntie calms the mare. Mother's voice, calm and clear in the storm: *little girl, little girl.* I limp, sob; but she makes me walk back to the hogan, says *Be strong, one day I won't be here to care for you.* Auntie rinses mud from my hair, Mother washes me with warm water and soap. Father bundles me in a wool blanket like a cradleboard baby. A dark purple bruise on my thigh, and always, the sensation of wings. Realizing for the first time that it will end one day—under the hooves of a spooked horse, a car accident, or like Mother with lung cancer eating away her life. I wanted to fly everywhere, all of the time.

I pick up coffee at a fast food drive-through near the old mall on the north side of Flagstaff; move slowly on sheets of ice. Snowflakes swirl from all directions beneath yellow lamppost lights. No pedestrians, few cars; the street I live on is constrained and empty. I use my foot to clear the front steps. The coffee cup slips from my hand, leaves a stain in the snow which might be wings or folded arms.

She tells the Twins to spare some of the monsters. Extended families, lovers, strangers; blue and red horses, coyotes. Hunger, poverty; uranium, cancer. Artifacts from the past and messages in the light of a setting sun; shifting stories, fluid and unfinished.

Inside the porch something hangs from the latch, rolled up in a sheet of artist's canvas: promising, threatening. An envelope, a note. A Storm Pattern blanket reflecting hundreds of miles of life.

ELLARAINE LOCKIE

If Women Ran the World

Hankies with holes and dried snot
hung as public assistance signs tied to a fencepost
in front of the house that bordered the railroad tracks
If wind whipped them into tumbleweeds
Notches carved in hobo shorthand in the wood
advertised the community service

My mother fried Spam in bacon grease
minutes after the five-fifteen screeched to a halt
The whistle having dinner-belled need for food
as dependably as the knock on the door
She squeezed the pink slices between buttered bread
that folded into recycled waxed paper
And delivered it to the man wearing whiskers
and filthy clothes waiting by the fencepost

Back then I saw it as charity
Even though Dad wore the look he did
when Mom made him go to church
The same look probably that Grandpa wore
when Grandma made pork sandwiches for Willow Stick
whenever he appeared on his pinto
at the edge of their homestead

Grandpa said *Woman, those Indians are gonna scalp you*
She built a bartering business with the Cree anyway
Homemade lye soap and pickled pigs' feet
for chokecherries and peace of mind
Grandma knew how to hold onto her hair

In California I offer the plumber, tree trimmer
and furnace repairman
homemade cinnamon rolls and coffee
My husband wants to know why
since we're paying them

LEAH HEDRICK

Remnants, Pt. III

"Women are 70 times more likely to be killed in the two weeks after leaving than at any other time during the relationship." - *Iowa DVIP*

two bones   broke in my right hand and healed   wrong

it still writes and packs and smokes   and moves

doesn't often   hurt anymore, but the fingers   kink

it clutches   wrong, index slanted over so the distal

knuckles crash   nail scrapes nail   they called it a

boxers' fracture but I was running   not fighting

when he slammed it   in the door I was trying   to close

Western Woman

She grew up here.

She knows the streets; the rundown
apartments, crowded buses, and subways.

She knows the fellas that shout their
ignorant cat calls; the females that stare her
down like territorial she-wolves looking
for a challenge.

She has no time for either.
She knows the inside of the office buildings—

The overload of shuffled documents,
waiting to be processed and passed on to this
attorney and that exec.

She knows the pink and orange sunsets that
fall beyond the horizon; the quiet beaches
with their soft, clean sand

and the crowded, noisy ones laced with
litter, breakdance competitions, and college
students trying to earn a buck.

Been close enough to touch that old
Hollywood sign in the mountainous
backdrop of the city.

She's sat with the homeless, listening to
them rant, or share a story; some of them too
drugged out
to recognize the warm coat laid across their
shoulders; and the ones who say to her,
Open dat Bible in yo' han,' Girl, read me
what Da Good Book say!

She knows the grocery stores with their
scuffed-up floors, not-far-off expiration
dates and limited selections—

the well-stocked markets with fine window
displays and assortments; shelves lined with
homegrown produce.

She knows the process at the airports—
from the removal of her shoes to the quart
sized baggie of toiletries.

She's traveled a bit, here and there. Met the kin. Seen some new places.

This place—with its rhythmic and impulsive
blends of colors and flavors; its fashion
trends, upbeat night life and overall intensity
will always hold a place in her heart. This is
where she was raised, taught
to take chances, and learned to persevere.

She moved away.

She knows this place; got drawn in—

to the green trees and rolling hills; the
brightly colored autumn foliage; rivers and
waterfalls.

She feels at home in this place.

She could breathe here, from the moment
her breath got swept away by windstorms
strong enough to bend the mighty pines;
and snowfalls gentle enough to catch in her
knitted mittens.

Here, she birthed her children and
memorized their laughter. Here, she heard
the voice of the God who drew her close,
taught her who she is, and breathed new life into her existence.

Here, she fell in love.

. . . Treasure

She is not like her older sister and older cousins, who hate visiting their grandparents' Los Corrales ranch while their mothers nurse newborns and their fathers irrigate the fields. They whine when Adelaida hands them baskets to gather breakfast eggs and complain when Abenicio asks them to churn butter. To the older children, the ranch is work. Hard work. They would rather be with their friends in Albuquerque—in the city. Not my mother. She opens the barn door to a trove of steel tongs, silver spurs, iron rods, and brass bells. She descends the cellar steps to jewel-toned jars of cherries, plums, apricots, and honey. To her, the ranch is a mystery, a miracle, and each day when her chores are done, she explores the grounds with Abenicio's empty tobacco bags gathering arrowheads, dandelions, prairie hawk feathers, rusty nails, buffalo head nickels, and shards of aged blue glass. Treasure pouches, she calls them, and draws tight the yellow strings.

ELLARAINE LOCKIE

Witches of the West

Stella slipped it through community control
camouflaged in a china cup and saucer collection
Her English immigrant mother's legacy
furnishing the logic for futuristic looks
at tea leaves clinging to each cup
after Ladies Aide luncheons

Even women who detested tea
would drink it at Stella's
Appear on her porch carrying a cooked-up
excuse of cookies or a gathering from their gardens
Hoping the symbols of connivance
wouldn't materialize in the contour
of a dreaded tea leaf cat
Or in the minister's Sunday morning sermon
when he likened sorcery to idolatry

The husbands were equally anxious
that the man of God might have heard
whispers of water witchery
The water-witch sitting beside me in the last pew
ready for our family's fast get-away
Should he have risen that week before the sun
and before a man in a pick-up
arrived with a slaughtered side of pork

Payment to my father
and his forked willow branch proficiency
to predict the fortune of a piece of parched prairie

A birthright he refused me
So that no tea leaves in the shape
of scandal's owl would stick to the sides
of my tea cup at Stella's
As though a father's sanction were essential
for blood knowledge to seep through soil

ANITA CRUSE

Sunflower Women

I hear the echoing hoofbeats
    down these winding sunflower highways.
The strides of the men on their road-weary horses
    the smell of sweat and leather and desperation thick with heat.

The women:
    Did they ride in a wagon?
    Wash their babes in the river?
    Weave flowers in their hair with fingers scented by sage?

Eyes fierce, head bowed, obedience,
    hands hard-cracked.
Do the washing, the mending, the feeding
    and the fixing.
Make supper with little for
    the men come home soon.

Were they beautiful?
    Were they loved?
    Did they ever ask "Who am I?" or "Why me?"
Or were such questions irrelevant
    under the frank, relentless sun?
With a family to feed, a man to please, animals to slaughter?
Crops to grow, house to keep, clothes to wash?
Did they do these things with thoughts of us?
The women:
    Farmers
    Ranchers
    The cowgirls to come
So that we may dream
    and loaf
    and drive our own tractor?

So that we may ride,
> and rope,
> and conquer that southwestern sun?

The years melt, she reaches out,
> and I grasp that woman's hand.

Her calluses connect with mine;
> feminine jigsaw of the West.

I feel her weariness,
> the faded sepia tone of her dreams
> she sees mine in technicolor
> and watches my pen move across the page.

Then she climbs back up in the wagon, gives the lines a twitch and is
> swallowed by the sage.

The sunflowers bend the breeze of her passing:
> The women who built the West.

ALBUM

CAROLYN DAHL

Emma's Seeds

Emma's daughters always marry
farmers' sons, boys with bulb-like hearts who are silent as seeds,
but promise fidelity deep as tap roots. To her romantic girls,

the boys are young lords with silver
plows, who open the underworld and prove an inheritance
of dark riches. Every summer, the boys' fields are gardens,

gold-tasseled corn, sweet purple
clover the girls nip for honey-filled cups, while under
their feet, potato plants grow small moons that glow

in the starless galaxy of Earth.
Junes pass like rosary beads. Julys move with the texture
of hymns, soft as the cottonwoods' windblown silk

settling in the girls' unbound hair.
The girls love the land and their young husbands, find no bondage
in the rhythm of daily labors. Still, they ask their mother: Does

all farm beauty bend to purpose?
Plums dangling like cabochons in orchard light, must we pluck
and can them in juice against winter's white starvation?

The pin-feathered yellow chick, peeping
softly in our palms, must it grow to an egg-laying hen? The big-eyed,
long-lashed calf who takes our hands in its toothless mouth to suck

some sweetness from its short life,
how can we release this tenderness to the destiny of market? Emma
knows this womanly sorrow and pulls onyx-eyed seeds from her apron.

Come spring in her daughters' gardens, the hard wombs
of poppies explode, burst with crinkled red petals, thin and brilliant
as tissue paper someone set on fire, burning in useless beauty.

When She Speaks

When my mother speaks, her hands fold in her lap like the wings of a pale bird. She leans back in her antique rocker and the amber light of her reading lamp shines in her bifocals like two rising moons. Her voice becomes a whisper. Her words drift through the room like the piñon incense smoldering from tabletop urns, caressing her display of relics—cowbells, coffee cans, railroad spikes, rosary beads—unlocking the stories within. When my mother speaks, I see relatives I have never met, walk ground I have never visited, inhabit memories not my own.

When my mother speaks, I dream.

DAVID LAVAR COY

Grandma's Apron

Kids, nowadays, have plumb forgot
how much use her apron got.
It kept the dress beneath it clean
It was potholder for hot beans
It dried the eyes of children's tears
and wiped the dirt out of their ears
it carried eggs and fussy chicks,
cleared the smoke when it was thick,
scared houseflies and errant bees
out of the room, held shelled peas.
It hid shy kids from strangers' eyes
and toted forth fresh cherry pies.
It mopped the sweat that wet her brow.
At dinnertime, amazing how
it brought the folks out of the field
when stoutly waved and proudly held.

CINDY L. PRATER

My Vietnam Blessing

Aunt Noi called me last night to tell me she has finished my quilt. She has also just finished one for my sister. She gleefully explained the pattern and fabric colors she chose for me, but with my limited understanding of quilting terms and her Thai accent, I'm not exactly sure what it will look like. What I do know from seeing her previous work is that the colors woven together will be bold and contrasting and her stitches will be nothing less than fine. Aunt Noi did relay quite clearly over the phone that the only way we can get our quilts is to come *home*.

Although she is officially retired, Noi continues to work at an assisted living home in Valentine, Nebraska, Monday through Friday mornings, her shift starting at 6:30 A.M. She has tried to quit, but her work ethic and the detailed diligence of her cleaning routine have yet to be satisfactorily replaced. She is also a favorite among the residents, whom she treats as lovingly as her own family.

On blustery Friday evenings, after gardens have gone to sleep and the rows of giant round prairie hay bales are aligned along fences, Noi's eldest daughter, Sheila, comes into town to pick her up. After mother and daughter admonish Uncle Jim to stay put and eat the healthy meal Noi pre-prepared for him, the two leave to spend the weekend quilting in the cozy basement of Sheila's ranch house. It's a scenic twenty-minute drive along U.S. highway 83, just across the South Dakota border and onto the Rosebud Sioux Indian Reservation. This rolling sand hills prairie, containing a few river-sliced canyons, is *home*.

My phone visit with Noi lasted over half an hour; we didn't only talk about the quilt. My tears were immediate as she shared how much she misses my mom, her late sister-in-law whom she affectionately called, Sis. I was proud of my control over my voice while I talked about how much I miss her, too. She also expressed concern over Uncle Jim's stubbornness and declining health. Her Thai-controlled phonetics is still quite strong after forty-plus years in America. She said of Uncle Jim's advanced diabetes: "He okay now, he scare me hap' to deah' in mornin', I shake, shake, he no wake up . . . he cold . . . low blu-sugar." At least now he can have his thrice-weekly dialysis done at the newly updated hospital in Valentine. They used to have to drive over forty miles to the Indian Health Services Hospital; diabetes is culturally prevalent in the wider reservation area.

Uncle Jim was an Army mechanic during the Vietnam War and was stationed in Thailand, where my cousin Sheila was born. I remember seeing her for the first time in a yellow-flowered vinyl and chrome stroller. Her thick dark hair, glossy under Grandma's florescent light, ended in a sweet curl at her shoulders. My younger brother and I sat on Grandma's crocheted bread-sack rugs in front of the stroller, doing whatever silly things we could think of to sustain her cherubic belly laughs. Noi was already pregnant with my cousin Tom at the time. Though she was in her twenties, I remember thinking that she looked like a little girl with a big-girl hairdo. I didn't think there was any way she could be pregnant because her tummy looked like she had slipped one of Grandma's smallest couch pillows from beside her and tucked it under her tropical print dress, just like my friends and I did when we were pretending to play house.

Noi entered my life when I was at that self-conscious yet invisible age. I was too old to be cute but not nearly old enough to sit with the grown-ups at the big oak table in the living room. Grandma's overly warm house in Valentine was small and *always* smelled of food cooking: coffee, bread, bacon, cookies, fried chicken, or pork chops, depending on the season and time of day. After leftovers were tucked away and the many crusty pans had been scrubbed clean, the women finally seated themselves around the blue-checkered oilcloth that covered her iconic white 1950s table. It had been a better fit in her kitchen on the farm. Though her town kitchen was a generous size in comparison to the rest of her house, it was made quite snug by the wringer washer and tub, the new Frigidaire "ice box," the propane heat stove, a wall of cupboards, and the propane cook stove. Bored, restless, ditched by older siblings who could drive around with friends, and tired of playing with the little kids, I had the choice of either seating myself on the living room carpet and keeping quiet while the men watched a snowy black-and-white football game, or hovering in the kitchen.

Conversing with the women at family gatherings was difficult for Noi those first few years. The women's conversation was out of my range, too, although for different reasons. Noi often brought handwork along and would sit crocheting or knitting while the other ladies chatted. Her busy hands piqued my interest.

Noi and I found companionship in each other as she taught me how to crochet. I had learned to cast-on and create a few simple knitted rows from Grandma and a friend's mother previously, but managing slick needles and the frustration of dropped stitches completely drained my desire to practice. This bit of experience did, however, give me an understanding of the properties of yarn. Noi gave me a hook and a small leftover red yarn ball and got me started. At the end of the first afternoon of lessons, I had proudly crocheted a lumpy and almost symmetrical square. We didn't need to speak each other's language to transfer and receive the lessons. Noi was left handed, I was right, so facing her worked well. If I didn't make a stitch correctly, a simple, "No, no . . . 'dis way" would suffice. She held her work closer to me and slowed the stitch formation down. I studied the movement of her hands more carefully and tried to imitate what she'd done. By the next holiday I was crocheting dolly blankets and by the next, tube dresses and skirts to slide naked Barbie dolls into. By the time I was in my early teens I was making lap robes and couch covers, and when I was a high school senior I crocheted my own shawl and purse for prom. Noi's hands guided mine into womanhood, as I made soft, fuzzy blankets to cradle my children and grandchildren in.

Noi did not stay quiet and shy for long around her extended family. As her kids grew, so did the volume of her voice and the number of words we could understand. "You ge' ove' here! I 'pank you ahh." Many of Noi's phrases were learned through Uncle Jim. Some were through trial and error, though I think Grandma did what she could to gently point out mistakes and correct errors in local social convention. One warm Easter afternoon, we were in Noi's fenced yard watching Sheila toddle around in the new grass carrying her plastic pink baby bottle. It was full of a dark liquid. "Is that prune juice?" One of the women asked. "Coke . . . she like it," Noi responded confidently. There was no awkward, embarrassing reprimand. I'm sure Grandma suggested a more appropriate beverage for a toddler during a private opportunity. As an adult I am grateful that I was able to have respect modeled in such a loving way. There were times we learned to accept things the way they were.

I received a birthday card from Noi one spring that read something like, "To a dear Aunt." My mother countered my young puzzlement with an honest explanation of Noi's ability to read English and the fact that it was a beautiful card and, even more importantly, a thoughtful act.

Noi has never meant to offend, though she has at times been blunt, and not a bit discreet with questions such as, "How you ge' so fat?" Of course she asks this while setting out an unbelievable selection of Thai and American dishes that she expects you to stuff yourself with. Even as she grows older, there is a sassy agelessness about her. Her whole being becomes animated with excitement when she sees you after months of absence.

I took the phone from my husband last night and heard, "How yoo, honey?" With both of my parents gone, hearing her familiar greeting made me feel the comfort of a child who is still loved and loved unconditionally. It suddenly doesn't matter that I didn't send a Christmas card this year or that I can't understand everything she says. It doesn't matter that she grew up in a remote village outside of Bangkok, and that a world conflict was the impetus for the grafting that brought her into our loving and less-than-perfect family tree. What does matter to me is that our conversation ended in "love yoo" and "love you too" and included the reminder that a very special gift is waiting for my return *home*.

GAIL DENHAM

Apron

Who knew that one day Mom's old apron, a bib
and short skirt, supported by frayed straps, tied
in the back, could hold so many memories?

Mom worked full-time as a bookkeeper in a lumber
mill, big industry here in this tiny western town—her
tiny precise numbers filling line after line in account
books. No computers.

I know now, her feet barely drug her in the back door
after staring at figures all day, her arthritic neck bent
over a desk. Yet her Finnish stubborn spirit prevailed.
She had to work—to care for her family.

Still, when she strapped on that apron, we knew our
supper would appear. She left the apron on for meals;
afterward, she might clean a bathroom, whip up an angel
food cake for church supper, or gather eggs.

She didn't sit much. Often the radio tuned to favorite
evening radio programs. We sat enthralled by "The Shadow
Knows" or "Fibber McGee" while Mom pulled out her big
yellow bowl with blue stripes and made cookies.

We kids tried to avoid dishwashing chores, but it was our job.
No dishwashers. Often I peeled and boiled potatoes before
she got home—small help, I'm sure, as I often left them
to burn, while I skipped out to play softball.

We fell asleep evenings listening to "Beulah" or "Science Theater;"
our noses twitched at cookie odors. I do think she hung up the apron
by the back door before she finally crawled into bed, exhausted.
I still use that precious apron.

SALLY CLARK

Homesteading in Paradise

The season's tomatoes picked,
red, ripe, and heavy as breasts,
die kinder beg to swim
in the shallow creek
behind the house
while the August sun bakes
their immigrant farm.

But Muti knows danger
slithers in narrow eyes and
angry cotton-mouths
lying in wait, hungry
for exposed flesh and
seeking vengeance.

Bat-guano powder and
hand-poured lead too costly
to be spent killing snakes,
and Vater in far away fields,
wrestling food from amongst
the thorns and thistles,
his arms bleeding from
tears in his flesh and
blisters on his hands,

the small woman sets aside
her boiling jars
waiting to be filled,
perspiration dripping from
her arms and neck and down
the backs of her legs,
absorbed briefly by her

faded cotton skirt, the
colors of her shirt
darkened and bleeding
into her skin.

Shouldering the hoe that
weeds the garden in
diminutive hands,
she clutches up
her skirts and her fears
to walk to the creek bed,
ignoring grass burrs grabbing
at her worn stockings,
spear grass arching
into her ankles.

Swallowing hard,
she sets about
to sever the heads of those
black, evil vipers, hungry
for her children's lives,
cold blood feeding
the dusty ground,
pungent corpses tossed
onto an open fire,
roasting flesh rising
like incense
to a cloudless sky.

Her task complete, she returns to
the house and works to
preserve the blood-ripe tomatoes
that will feed her family through
the coming winter, pausing
occasionally to listen for
the distant sound of

careless laughter, of
gentle, baptismal splashes
carried on a quiet,
summer breeze.

RICK KEMPA

A Circle of Family

for Fern Callen

The picture is familiar to us all:
Grandma out in the garden leaning on her hoe,
squinting through the dust raised by our approach,
lifting her arm in greeting, then
bending back down to finish off a row.

How astonishing that garden was!
Year after year, despite killer frosts, locusts,
hailstorms, it yielded under her care
bushels of potatoes, corn, tomatoes, turnips, peas . . .
Our mouths water just to think of it.

Once when we were snapping beans, I asked,
"Grandma, how do you do it? What's your secret?"
She shrugged, said something matter-of-fact
like *anything grows if you water it,*
but the truth is, as we all know,
that she coaxed every plant in that garden to life.
That was her special gift: to love the life in every seed,
in the fluttering heart of every bird, in every child's eyes.
And everything responded to her love.

A lucky thing, to be born a kitten on the Point Ranch,
and to learn that every afternoon without fail,
her cry would ring out, *Here kitty, kitty, kitty*!
and on a platter by the front gate
you would find more than you could eat.

A happy life, to be a flower in that little patch of earth
outside her door, to have her stand above you
and admire you. Wouldn't you do your best
to strain toward the light, to bloom for her?
Gesturing with her cane, she'd say, "Patty gave me
the rose. The marigolds came from Erma Lee.
Joy brought the lavender bells up from Tucson."

And that gallery of pictures on her icebox,
all those children's faces smiling out at us:
You could point to any one and ask,
"Now who's this, grandma?" and she would give
not just the child's name and age, but who he or she
"belonged to," and a story or two as well.
She kept track of us all.

We've all known the pleasure of her living room,
being together around her, the aroma of roast
permeating the air, the TV off, the talk
turning this way and that, the laughter
ringing out, the kids huddled behind the sofa
with her famous bag of toys. We could sit there
all day; we could sit there forever. We may not have
known it at the time, but we know now:
we were as close to home as we will ever get.

In the forest there are certain trees which multiply
not through their seeds, but by their roots.
Saplings range out on all sides, maturing,
sprouting seedlings of their own until
the one who spawned them all is lost to view.
If you work your way through thickets of new growth
to the center, you will find an emptiness there,
a blank space where the mother tree once stood.

This is how it is with us. Because of Fern,
we are all connected, a circle of family
with her love, her love for life, alive in each of us.
And although today the absence in our center
makes us grieve, the deeper truth, the one
that will emerge throughout the years, is this:
Grandma is not gone, she lives within us.

. . . Rosewater

Pick fresh petals. Fill up your skirt. But gather no stems or leaves. Come back to the kitchen and rinse out the bugs and fill the saucepan with petals. A few inches deep. Pack them gently. Put water on the stove and wait until it's steaming but not boiling. Good. Now pour the water over the petals until they're covered. Put the lid on the pan and let it steep until the water turns pink and the petals turn white and oil drops bead on the surface. Strain the pan with a colander. Press down on the petals with a spoon. Pour the juice in a jelly jar. This is rosewater, Adelaida tells my mother. Splash some on your hands and face. Now you are clean.

KATHLEEN WINTER

Mean Time, Prime Time

From behind a vintage apron I mine the future,
my instrument one silver-plated spoon.
It's tomorrow in Europe—
can it be yesterday anywhere now?

Above our kitchen sink this shell's
a month from chill sand where it washed up,
its home beach a nation away from my hands.
Where's the farthest a person could be ahead of us?
Where's the farthest she could be now, behind?

For your answer, stand fast in the right place
in time, smack in the middle between yesterday,
tomorrow. What do you think of when you wake
there in the center of the night?

Good nights, the hope I might grow kinder.
Grim nights, of families forcibly estranged,
mean times, too vivid traces of the losses
we're terrified to wake of.

Mean life is the average time a particle
(unstable particle) survives before decay.
Mean length of utterance, the middle watch,
night soil, these things to fertilize or scarify the mind.

Still in our prime, we lie in the moon's tow.
I wind around your sleep, my limbs
the nameless shade inside your shell.
Sweep me in your pacific, breathing tide
toward deeps in the here, the now.

CAROLYN DAHL

Boss Over the Bull

With a head hard as the horns they sawed away, the breeding bull shoves the young girl against the stall wall, marking her thin chest with the circle of its nose ring.

> *You're going to have to teach it who's boss,* her father says.

The bull bangs the stanchion lock against the worn-out post of the stall, shredding the wood into slivers the wasps will collect later for their nests.

The girl is eleven years old. She hasn't become boss of herself yet and wonders how she can teach 800 pounds of bull that she, still a child, rules its life, is its boss, when it could grind her body down like silage. She'd heard the stories of crazed bulls, mean with a need for the heifers waiting in the pasture. Last week, one went mad at the neighbor's, charged a cow with a new calf, throwing the baby into the air, then trampling it to death. The rancher had to shoot the bull to save the other calves in the herd.

> *Here's what you do,* her father says. *Hide in the haystack*
> *near the water tank. When the bull comes to drink, jump up*
> *and hit it hard between the eyes with a strong length of pipe.*

How easy her father makes it sound. But she's old enough to know a bull's terrifying power. What if he charges and she can't make it to the fence? What if the wasps in the hay sting her? What if she freezes and can't strike quickly, or she doesn't hit the bull hard enough to stop him? If she dared, she'd tell her father she doesn't want to hit an animal. She doesn't want to be boss of anything.

> *Honey, I'll be at the fence with the gun,* her father says.
> *If you don't do it. That bull's going to kill you eventually.*

The girl didn't sense that the bull hated her, just liked to shove her around to show his muscles. But her father knew animals, how sometimes one will have it in for a person without reason. If she objects, he'll only lift up his pant leg and show her his crooked leg as proof.

The bull is the most dangerous animal we own, her father reminds her.

The girl has been taught to do what her father says, so she hides in the hay stack and waits, pipe in hand. The bull thunders into the barnyard, shaking the ground under her trembling legs. It lifts its head and smells her in the hay-scented air. It snorts, paws the dirt throwing dust clouds over its fur-raised back. Fed by terror, the girl springs up sooner than she had planned and runs toward the bull. It charges with a lowered head. The girl raises the pipe as high as she can to gather force and hits the bull between the eyes. Its skull is so hard, the pipe bounces back at the girl as if she'd hit concrete. She falls to the ground, the pipe slips from her hand and rolls away.

The bull staggers to one side. Its eyes roll back to the whites. It falters as if about to collapse on its knees, but rights itself, turns away from the girl, and stumbles out of the barnyard as if it weren't sure how many legs it had and how to make them work together.

Who's boss now? her father says, laughing.

From then on, whenever the girl enters the pasture to collect the heifers, she always carries the pipe. The bull hangs at the edge of the herd and eyes her with distrust. The girl doesn't know if the bull believes she is boss now and fears her, or if he simply waits for the perfect moment to strike back. The girl knows she deserves his hatred. Pain isn't the way to rule an animal's heart, and not even her father can read an animal's mind and know its intent.

On Christmas Eve her father tells the story to all the relatives, talking about her bravery, how she's as tough as any boy and showed the bull who's boss all right. But the girl slips away to the barn, hoping the myth she'd heard is true. The old timers say that at midnight, all the animals, even the bull, drop to their knees and bow down to a child.

GUST

ANNIE LAMPMAN

My Galapagos

She soars arms outstretched to sky, embraces
the roll and heft of empty fields, skims larkspur
wheat silk that waves her passing glide—dais
for cricket, horse fly. Only her lover

sees her lone spiral to furrowed
earth. She covers herself with dappled shroud
streams ribbons of dust, garlands the fir
with mourning, wraps herself tight, dowry

of light and dust she brings to him, opens
her flight and pulls him in looping curve,
follows river gulch, shored ocean
dips low through virga of cloud and current.

Undressed by the wind and sea they fly naked,
Eclipse the thunder of the earth's making.

BETSY BERNFELD

Bleeding in the Wilderness

I've read that women should stay out of the wilderness
during their periods. It infuriates the bears.

Stepping into the woods
air thick with humidity
slurp of water, hint of breeze
not necessarily the sweet scent of flowers
but more basic, instinctual smells
leaves, pollen, mud.
I will never be a naturalist
recording the dates when each species blooms
let alone plucking a sample for the herbarium
or shooting a bird so it can become
a famous painting. The sight
of a wild rose is irrational, erotic.
Sniffing its center I am alive and once again,
bleeding.

During the thirteen-hour ascent of Mt. Nez Perce,
off route, roped up, unable to release
the climbing harness to change a pad
and so bleeding down my legs
soaking through thick Air Force pants
all the way to the knees,
retching on the summit, regaining control
with measured breaths and small bits
of chocolate in my mouth,
rappelling down a waterfall
now wet also from outside in,
dragging home over blowdown trees
plastic bags of bloody garments.

Wandering three days from Rendezvous Peak to Hurricane Pass
sunburned, swollen, pounding headache,
studying high alpine flora, keying and classifying
in blinding light, never learning
one yellow composite from another
or identifying the penstemon,
peeing on miniature tundra flowers,
my knees like elephants, feeling the release
of the fertilized ovum and then plunging down
Avalanche Canyon pouring copious blood and tears
finally at Bradley Lake empty and thin
remembering only the forget-me-nots.

Walking carefully in the dark toward the Grand Tetons,
sensing again the presence of small innocent company,
nibbling Underwood deviled ham on Wheat
Thins crackers, less nauseous as we passed
timberline and entered onto the rocks at 4 A.M.,
climbing guides ahead and above us
swinging their headlamps calling to clients,
edging past frightened tourists on Wall Street,
feeling at home on all the familiar pitches,
rejecting the free rappel on the descent,
instead hugging rough rock all the way down.

Laboring thirteen hours again
this time in the hospital a long wet birth
sucking chips of ice
taking in tiny increments of air
my stomach a mountain
each pain jagged
lasting three minutes hour
after bloody hour unable to speak
don't touch me
don't touch my bed swooping upward
toward a summit

walking off the gentler side.
My husband, the naturalist,
keeping time, writing notes for the doctor.
Under bright lights before anesthetic
delivering in rhythmic breaths
and wild uncontrolled bleeding.

The sun is coming up later now,
I am lazier, too.
The forest is full of goldenrod, fireweed, cone flowers
tall and solemn and most
ominous of all the purple fleabane.
Clouds of pine pollen are long settled,
today's haze is from Idaho fires
fertilization long over, flowers
coalescing to seeds
mellow bears plucking tiny huckleberries.

The Swallows

Every day Grandma sat in her chair by the window and complained how the swallows built their nests right under the eaves. "Look at those birds with their dirty little britches," she'd say. I wanted more than anything to please her; I was, after all, wooing her granddaughter, and while I did not ask her consent, I craved her blessing. And so every day I'd get up on a ladder and clean the shit and feathers from the window. That helped, but not enough; still she complained about the birds.

One afternoon when she went into town I figured I'd surprise her, so I got out the broom and climbed up there, and I beat at the nests until they cartwheeled down. Then came the hard part, for which I wasn't prepared— to get rid of the bald little babies flopping around on the lawn. The thought that I was doing it for her made it easier to smack them with a shovel and scoop the whole mess over in the tallgrass, and I admit I felt a manly rush as I did this: I was a regular ranch hand taking care of business, not some soft city poet.

In the evening, when Grandma shuffled over to her chair, she asked at once, "Where are the swallows?"

I said with a smile, "Grandma, I took care of them for you."

"What do you mean *took care of them*?" she said, and there was something in her voice that made my heart beat faster. "What about the babies?"

"But Grandma," I said, "I thought you wanted . . ." I stopped, seeing how she cocked her head to peer up under the eaves, and how her shoulders slumped when she saw the nests were gone. She sat there for a long time without speaking, not napping like she always does, and when dusk came and there were no swallows veering and darting outside her window, bringing back insects for their babies, we grew completely miserable, I the killer, she accomplice, watching the light retreat across the empty fields into the big sky.

ANNIE LAMPMAN

A Mother's Guide to Birds and Boys

The first rule is simple: Look at the bird. ~ The Sibley Guide to Birds

Sometimes the pairings are a surprise: a burbling trill quickly connected to shape and color of feather and beak—the song, the bird, the name, a hidden bit of knowledge I didn't realize I possessed. Others—a robin's sleepy burble, the finch's scolding chatter—are so familiar they are no more a surprise than morning light streaming in the bedroom window or wind moving through the trees. Ubiquitous narration to outside's constant movement: the buzz of a bee, a cricket's rasp, a swallow's chirp, a hawk's distant *cheeeeawv.*

The birds I know by sight and sound make a short list, but there is a rhythm to their names, an implied music to their pairings: *flicker, dipper, nuthatch, chickadee, cat bird, canyon wren, humming bird, house finch, horned owl, meadowlark, mourning dove, magpie, mocking bird, mallard, killdeer, pheasant, seagull, grosbeak, robin, blackbird, Steller's jay, cowbird, quail, crow, starling, swallow, red tail, grouse, junco, osprey, raven.* Not so many, but enough to feel connected, to track their movements and songs, to rejoice at their sudden showings in the backyard spruce or privet or apple trees; on a walk along the Snake River's basalt bluffs, muddy shore, and bunch grass slopes; or in the pines or cattails or willow scrub of the rolling prairie north-Idaho college town where I live with my husband and three sons.

Sometimes—when a bird lands close by, its song clear and loud as it sits perched on some branch or bluff or grass bunch—I greet it back, cawing or whistling my approximation of whatever its call is. With a sideways tilt of head, it takes me in before singing again, fervently communicating love or territorial warning or afternoon sun joy—things I can feel and understand. But no matter how much I may think I know about them, may want to know about them, when it comes down to it, I'm just a ground-dweller longing for sky. Held aground by the gravity and weight of Earth's constant movement, flightless.

*

Growing up in the woods of north-central Idaho, surrounded by nothing but nature all the way to Canada and back, my mother taught me birds and trees and flowers, just as her mother—a bonsai artist, master flower arranger, and horticulturist—taught her. I learned early to train my ears and eyes to recognize the divine: a leaning larch anchored root to rock in graceful reach; a stunted alpine spruce; a clump of fireweed blooming bright against a cut bank; mountain chickadees singing their own names; a catbird in the front yard calling, *Hey Mary, Hey Mary*; a flicker winging by, white rump flashing; the resident town heron, heavy winged and blue. The juvenile red-tail kicked from its nest, circling overhead in its brown-and-white feather patchwork, landing clumsily in our maple tree, crying *pwee pwee* for its mother, seeking her familiar comfort.

*

I was a quiet, lonely child—a strange mix of only child, but with two older half-siblings on either parental side, whom I either was never around as a child, or wished I wasn't. I grew up playing by myself, daydreaming and reading books by the dozens. With our pet parakeet, I would listen to story records, turning the pages of the books that followed along: *Lady and the Tramp, Cinderella, Snow White and the Seven Dwarfs*. I would go outside and sit for hours on the front lawn, hoping that if I were still enough, the little chipmunks and songbirds would flock to me as they did with Cinderella—befriending me, sitting perched on my shoulder, twittering in my ear. That together, best of friends, we would embark on wondrous adventures.

But playing alone has its limitations. And woodland creatures, even little songbirds, tend to shy away from even the most earnest and quiet of little girls. When my mother was too busy to keep me company and the silent faces of my dolls and bears left me wishing for more, I would sometimes let myself picture what happy adventures I might have had if only my would-be twin would have survived. This twin wasn't just a lonely child's wishful thinking: at my birth, the doctor informed my mother that there was an accompanying undeveloped embryo in the womb with me. A sibling who, to me, was always and nothing but an identical twin sister.

I find myself thinking about the change a twin sister would have brought to my life more than ever now as I round the bend to forty, married for over two decades and mother of three nearly grown sons.

Twenty years of living in a one-female, four-male household, and I am a woman very much alone in a world of men. Of the hyper-masculine, alpha variety, my husband and three sons like to push themselves and take risks, obliterate the boundaries. My boys were boys who jumped from rooftops and treetops when they were hardly past toddlerhood, boys who even now launch themselves into the air at every opportunity—on mountain bikes, motorcycles, snowboards, wakeboards, surfboards, and in cars. Boys who are happy with the airborne weightlessness of a swan dive off of forty-foot-high rocks into the dark water below, arms outstretched to the sky for breathless, heady seconds. Boys who like speed and action and danger, who seek to find the limitations of their bodies every step of the way—their growth a battleground of cuts and scrapes, bruises and scars. They are boys who don't understand the feminine, whose softest touches are often still rough, who would rather do just about anything other than deal with female emotions they don't comprehend. I've learned to hang on for dear life, to hold my breath, to not watch when I know it will be more than I can bear. I've learned to be tough enough to stay calm, to inhabit their world as fully as I can—so that I might try to teach them mine.

When my sons were young and developed an inexplicable fear of worms, I tried to demonstrate worms were nothing to be afraid of by plucking a few from the dirt, cupping them in my palm, and explaining the important work they did for the ecosystem—tilling and fertilizing the soil, and providing good nutrition, especially for birds. But no matter what I said, my sons' fears wouldn't be stemmed, so finally I selected a nice earthworm specimen, wiped it clean, casually popped it in my mouth, and ate it. My husband wouldn't kiss me for days, but I won my boys' awe and respect.

*

Like my mother and grandmother before me, I worked to instill in my sons an affinity for the natural world—a fascination with flight, with mysterious growth, with nature's movement, even though I knew the dangers and sorrows those things could bring.

When my sons got their first BB guns, then shotguns and .22s with scopes, I taught them about songbirds and raptors, ravens and water fowl, impressing upon them the singular beauty, vulnerability, and value of these birds, admonishing them to never, never shoot any of them. But as much as I knew my sons wanted to listen to me, to do right, I understood they would eventually crave more than paper bulls-eyes and cans, that whether I liked it or not they would find live targets. So I gave them free reign—I told them that not only were they allowed, but *encouraged* to shoot as many starlings as they could. I explained that European starlings were an invasive species pushing out native songbirds, that there were too many in our area, that, in this case, it was okay to shoot a bird. But in giving them permission, I also knew that starlings would be savvy opponents with their wary survival skills—that they would, in fact, be nearly impossible for the boys to successfully "hunt." And indeed they were. My sons spent years stalking starlings, sneaking around nesting sites, staking out the front yard or trees the birds frequented, but in over a decade of starling hunting, they only successfully shot one or two birds.

When my husband took our sons grouse hunting, they examined their slain quarry with a mix of sorrow and pride; when they had to gut, pluck, and eat the tiny carcass, I knew my lessons had been absorbed.

*

For a Mother's Day tribute on Facebook, a colleague recently shared a picture of his mother holding he and his twin sister as newborns, writing of the bond he and his twin shared, and even though I never got to have the experience, my heart ached. Had whatever it was—some genetic curse, some limitation of maternal blood supply, some quirk in the universe—not limited my existence to only me, who would I have become? Had my twin instead accompanied me on the lonely journey of my childhood, had we been friends and sisters, connected in that way only those who share a womb can be connected—developing together every step of the way, making decisions together, growing up together—who would I be now?

On hard days—days where the masculine in my life outweighs the feminine by more than quadruple, where the scales tip so sharply I'm not sure I can ever balance my way back—I think about her, my twin sister who would have understood what it means to be this woman—this daughter, this sister, this friend, this wife, this mother of three sons turning into teens turning into adults. Who would have understood better than anyone else what it means to be me.

But there is only me and my family of men. I've had to come to terms with that.

*

A few springs ago, inspired by an early Snake River duck-watching walk with a friend who loves birds as much as I do (and ducks even more), I researched and ordered a nice set of birding binoculars, along with the bird book she carried: *The Sibley Guide to Birds*—the requisite North American identification text. Together on that walk, passing her binoculars back and forth, we spotted a rare nesting pair of Merlins, spied wood ducks and mergansers and buffleheads, watched cinnamon teals and loads of coots.

I thought, perhaps with my new birding equipment, I would turn into a real birder—take it up as an obsession, eyes turned always upward, cataloging, memorizing, mimicking—adding to my repertoire of song and sight until the species I knew numbered into the hundreds. I started a life list, once more transformed into that girl sitting perched and hopeful in the front yard.

After my binoculars and bird book came, my husband and I would drive to a small local reservoir where I would instruct him to paddle our canoe quietly closer to flocks of migrating ducks as I kept my new binoculars steady, trying to differentiate between a common goldeneye and a Barrow's goldeneye, a greater scaup from a lesser scaup, marveling over the breeding colors of northern shovelers, ruddy ducks, and redheads.

My friend and I took little field trips to ponds full of migrating species, binoculars glued to our faces, stumbling down banks to get closer, paging through Sibley's until we were sure we had it—triumphant in our identification successes. I would come home excited to tell my family what we'd spotted. But after the spring's migration waned, my interest did, too. Without the thrill of new discovery, there was no need for identification work. *There's a robin. There's a hawk. There's a crow.* Everything I saw, familiar.

When a family trip to Ecuador came up, I was excited for the chance to see so many new, unfamiliar birds. I ordered *The Birds of Ecuador*—a thick brick of a book I carted with me, along with my binoculars, to the tiny Ecuadorian fishing village where we stayed for eight weeks. I paged through the new bird book, marveling, picking the birds of my dream life list: the blue-footed booby, the Andean cock-of-the-rock, the green honeycreeper, the paradise tanager, the hoatzin, the jabiru. Wild parrots flying free and raucous.

My sons rolled their eyes at me—binoculars again glued to my face, stumbling around outside, excitedly pointing and frantically paging through my bird book while the locals watched me with amusement. Each time I heard a new bird call I went running, determined to capture as many species as possible on my newly expanded list. *Did you see that!* I would demand, and my sons would look obediently and nod, forgetting the name as soon as I said it, but I hoped eventually, if I kept reminding them, some bit of knowledge might stick.

One broiling midday, coming back from surfing, the boys found a blue-footed booby lying on the beach, immobilized, attracting the attention of scavenging feral dogs. They scooped the bird up in towels and brought it home. A blue-footed booby in our backyard—one of the Ecuadorian species I'd been most excited to possibly see, and one whose name even the boys knew (not surprising, with the word "*booby*" involved). We named it Bluebell, tried to keep it out of the sun, tried to revive it with water, bought it fish we thought it might eat, but it would only rest for a moment, then stagger about drunkenly, those fantastic blue feet slapping against the hot concrete. Despite our best efforts, the bird continued to ail and died the next day.

Over the next few weeks, we found three more on the beach in the same state. We were devastated, but none of the locals seemed to notice. After a while, even the most exotic birds become familiar: *there's a caracara, there's a booby, there's a jabiru.*

*

A year later, back home in Idaho, I ask the boys what they remember about Ecuador.

They remember the big waves, the surfing, their trips around town on a motorcycle. They remember their movement, the action. The risk and adventure.

I ask them if they remember the way the water bubbled and held them aloft, if they remember the smells of night, the taste of the air, the way trees in the backyard filled with birds.

I ask them: *Do you remember the magnificent frigate birds, the croaking ground doves, the flocks of tiny green parrotlets? Do you remember Bluebell?*

Yes, they say. *Yes.* And I know, at least this once, they do.

*

When my sons were still very young, we kept parakeets. My mother had a parakeet when she was young, as did I. But unlike their mother and grandmother, my boys were frightened of the colorful, chattering birds. I have pictures of them—our green and blue and yellow budgies sitting on the tub faucet as the boys took a bath, both species wary of the other. Those little beaks that could so easily take chunks out of chubby fingers. Those little hands that could so easily wound a delicate wing.

Little boys grew, and parakeets turned into orange-cheeked cockatiels that sat uneasily atop tousled heads. Years passed, boys turned into teens, and cockatiels turned into an African Grey parrot who trusted only me, who kept a wary eye on tall boys, who in turn kept wary eyes on him—that beak big enough to lop off even a man's finger, those hands big enough to disable even strong wings.

They say African Greys are like having a perpetual two-year-old in the house—all of their sixty-year life span. Wanting of attention, jealous with affection. At turns sweet and loving. At turns angry and frightened. Both indifferent and needy. They say what you see in your two-year-old child is the same thing you'll see in them as a teen. That teens are just as needy as toddlers—just as longing for attention and keen for affection. At turns angry and withdrawn. At turns sweet and loving. Indifferent and sensitive.

Both boys and birds lash out, wound themselves, injure the ones they love. Both boys and birds suffer nightmares of falling, of helplessness, of finding themselves in the dark. Both boys and birds cry out for their mothers, burrowing into the comforting warmth they offer, flocking to the safety of their care, trusting in their groundedness. Even both boys and birds must sometimes surrender to the gravity and weight of Earth's constant movement.

They come to me—my boys who are now nearly men. They come to me with their broken hearts, with their worries about the future. They come to me for advice, to ask what they should do, which path they should take, what the right thing is. They come to me, and I give them a gentle nudge to take flight again.

*

On the same Snake River canyon walk I'd taken the year before with my friend, my husband and I watched a female bald eagle and her juvenile early in the spring. The juvenile flew to a low tree branch right above us and, in his clumsy landing, dropped the catfish his mother had caught for him. The fish plopped at our feet like a gift—talon-scarred but whole. I wanted to throw it back, help them reclaim it somehow. I didn't want the mother's hard work to go to waste—this feeding of her young, this rearing into adulthood so critical to the juvenile's survival. But the juvenile flew off. His mother met him in the sky and I could imagine her scolding him, but then, in some kind of bonding, or flying practice, or other bird inspiration I can only guess at, they grabbed talons midair and cartwheeled right above us—a sudden and fast rotation of wings and bodies, a momentum of circular falling so dramatic I clutched my chest and held my breath. They spun together at breakneck speed, heading for the river, spinning, spinning, until I was sure they would crash headlong into the water and perish. Only at the last minute did they separate, wingtips brushing river surface as they lifted themselves in heavy, sure strokes back to the air, the juvenile as strong as his mother and, hopefully, just as likely to survive—flourish even—despite his clumsy handling of his mother's hard work.

*

Chronicled in the book *Last Chance to See*, author Douglas Adams goes in search of one of New Zealand's famous flightless birds: the critically endangered kakapo—a fat, green-brown, nocturnal parrot, a feathered and winged ground-dweller that booms its love song out across mountaintops for everyone to hear. Adams writes: *There is something gripping about the idea that this creature has actually given up doing something that virtually every human being has yearned to do since the very first of us looked upward [. . . but] it's not merely the fact that it's given up that which we all so intensely desire, it's also the fact that it has made a terrible mistake which makes it so compelling.*

It seems we all long to fly, but in surrendering, do we, like the kakapo who came to the brink of non-existence in giving up its wings, endanger ourselves, or do we instead find a new existence, a loud kind of booming love? Do we find our own way to survive?

*

I keep quizzing them, my boys who are almost men. "*What bird is that?*" I ask in the voice I used with them when they were young—a tone meant to inspire curiosity and the excitement of discovery. Bird nests that had tumbled from trees, pieces of broken shells left behind from the hatching—a collection of found treasures. I still keep the remnants of those years displayed on a shelf: two tiny nests woven out of fluff; two severed hawk's feet; an intact crow skull with its shiny black beak; a robin's blue egg; three small brown-and-white specked eggs that will always remain unhatched.

But my sons are still largely disinterested in the games of birdcall or branched silhouette identification. I'm lucky to get a cursory glance, a little nod of acknowledgement. They know a basic few, and that's it: *starling, robin, swallow, crow, humming bird, bald eagle, hawk, osprey, mallard, pheasant, quail, grouse.* Their ear might turn toward a familiar song, but they don't know what bird made it. They might recognize something in flight, but they can't name it. But there's still time, I remind myself. They surprise me sometimes with a passing comment, a hidden bit of bird knowledge they too possess. "*Flicker, dipper, nuthatch, swallow,*" I whisper, pointing, waiting for them to say, *Yes.*

. . . Empty Spaces

Gathering kindling one morning, she and her grandfather hear a mewling from the woodpile. Abenicio moves aside a piñon log to reveal a sickly orange kitten. My mother scoops it up. Abenicio frowns. He does not need another hungry mouth. Maybe it's better to let nature takes its course. When she nuzzles the newborn to her cheek, he relents, so long as she cares for the stray herself and promises to understand if it does not survive. She makes a nest of rags behind the chicken coop and carries over a tin of cream. The kitten purrs. The next sunrise, my mother returns to find the rags scattered and the saucer upturned. Coyotes, Abenicio says, hand on her shoulder. Try to understand. It is the nature of things. Returning the rags to the barn, she pauses at a whimpering from the workbench. Under the stool, she discovers the watchdog, a yellow hound that had given birth to stillborn pups a week before, nursing the bony stray. At first my mother is puzzled by the wondrous thing—the union of opposites, how empty spaces somehow fill—but then she remembers her grandfather's words. She fluffs the rags into a cushion and smiles.

TORN

GAIL DENHAM

Lonely Vigil in Colorado

"Holding down the fort" means
feeding stock in five-degree weather
with Old Jake, the truck's shaky lights
focused on the barn door.

"Holding down the fort" is breaking
ice to water chickens; it's shattering
frozen long johns and diapers off
the line after the light's run out.

"Holding down the fort" means chopping
twice the wood Sunday night, cause
the butcher comes Monday, biscuits aren't
made, and how will you round up the pigs?

"Holding down the fort" is watching
soft snow fill the barn path, your footprints
circling the corral, remembering how it was,
knowing the beauty is gone.

"Holding down the fort" is every time
you pass a window, or feed animals,
you search the horizon, scraping
away frozen tears.

"Holding down the fort" is silent dinner
for three, uneven, facing the empty
space, willing food to slide down
your dry, cry-ready throat.

"Holding down the fort" means Sam Jr.
and Susie need more from you than you've
got left. You feed and water them, but turn
from their hungry looks.

"Holding down the fort" is carrying
a hot brick to warm clammy sheets
you aren't ready to wash yet, since then
his familiar smell would be gone too.

JESSICA MCDERMOTT

An Only Daughter Walks with Her Father

I
Along the abandoned road,
at the bottom of Idaho, where my dad
plans to die, we stumble upon hotpots

in an empty field. Where steam meets
breath he challenges me to touch with
a single finger. Feel where Shoshone

bathed in winter, where my ancestors
raked lake bottoms with work-horses,
where, should I go from here? From this

place of memories seeping like winter
runoff, where my dad parks the truck
and tells me he remembers the florescent

moss and hot water, here, we touch water
too hot to feel.

II
The family dump brimming
with forgotten trash: handlebars, mason jars,
tin cans, tires where trees should stand.

What did he hope to find here—
where hawks track kittens and cattle
drink from creek beds, where he sleeps

in his bully-barn with the door open
to hear the lost robins.

III

After he lost his thoughts, his ability
to remember, where Alzheimer's
sets in, without a word. Here, he becomes

first snowfall over the valley, hushed
earth, heavy sky. He tells me the horse
he had as a child was named Hawk,

asks where his dead wife is sleeping.
He becomes his mother who suffered
the same illness, and I become guilt

for the fights, for my not calling
or writing or visiting enough. Here,
family land becomes him. Walking

along forgotten fence lines we find the apple tree
his dad claimed to have planted at his birth.

Standing beneath untrimmed branches he reaches
up, grasping for apples I cannot see.

The Darkest

Brace your arms against both sides, where there's nothing to hold on to." Joy.

My butt slid off the ledge and I placed a tentative foot out against one side of the horizontal stem, two blank walls of limestone. My seat felt comfortable, indolent. I wanted to stay here and hang out, tell jokes and work up to the move, but my friends were quick. My extended leg wobbled. Ahead, Joy's boyfriend, Harsh, waited, face distant as the ripples of full moon reflected in running water. He didn't look worried about me; maybe my uncertainty stayed more concealed than I thought it did. It felt like every move I made was too weak to work the gravity-defying magic that I knew it would if I worked hard and trusted enough. Possibly Harsh didn't care enough to worry about my balance, but that was an ugly thought, down in this cave with the two of them. Frozen, unsure of my next move, I felt my leg grip, and knew I had to make my decision. I flexed my other foot, the one still planted on solid ground, slowed my breath, and tried again to scooch my body out into the chasm below by repositioning my grip and working my weight against both sides of the rock. But when I tried to move myself into the last few inches of the move, nothing happened. I just couldn't go.

Joy watched me, hawk-like. Before she could offer some idea that I'd have to try, I slid back to solid ground and tried to unclench. "I'm not feeling this," I said. "I might wait here." She narrowed her eyes, her smile bobbing from behind the poly-blend of Harsh's mud-caked plaid shirt.

"No," she said. "You can do it."

Joy and her pastel helmet, Harsh's perfect face. Down here, they knew who they were. "I can," I lied. "Not sure it's worth it, though. I'm really more interested in that last room. I can wait for you two back there." I gestured with my gloved hand, brushing the wall, and then patting it, apologetic to the lost shards of crystal for all they cared about being damaged.

Harsh raised one of his eyebrows. "I don't think we should split up," he said, his body still half-facing the dark ahead. Joy had moved into it. I shook my head.

"It's fifteen feet away, and you guys have to come back out this route. I'll wait." I'd have said *Just don't die*, but with his girlfriend already off again into the blackness, that didn't seem funny, even inside my head. "I'll wait down at the cavern, before the last climb," I said again. Harsh nodded: "Got it," and he was gone.

I was alone in the dark. We should have stayed together, with only three of us, and we knew this, but neither he nor she nor I suggested it. I beamed my headlamp into the space where they'd disappeared for a while, watching the light dwindle into ink, resting my spine against the rock and listening to the fast-fading thuds and murmurs. Then I turned to face my way back down the tunnel. Solo, the downclimb they had talked me though felt familiar and awkward. With only my headlamp, I had to pause at every step to shine my light down to see the footholds, think it out, then look back up as I took the step—but here, with no imminent risk of death if I slipped, my points of contact and my psyche stayed solid.

My climb: the first part involved what I can only describe as a slinky move between upper and lower body. The lower half of me sprang one direction and the other half stretched opposite-ways, this to avoid a massive chunk of inverted limestone where the downclimb opened itself. Once I got my feet lower, and my upper body past the chunk, there came a series of delicate stair steps. Alone, there was no margin for error, but no pressure to perform. I had no reason for a fall, and I didn't waver. At the bottom of my small solo victory, I'd entered a cave cavern, a room. I looked around. There were gaps below my feet, but none so large as to be dangerous. Just dark spaces between rocks. I found the rock seat where Harsh had taken pictures of Joy and me.

I rested.

For the first time since I'd passed the snake outside Bell's locked grate, I realized how sore and tired my legs and arms had become from bracing themselves and twisting around strange shapes. Shining light all around me, I admired cavern walls knobby and whorled with layers of seep and drip, abstract formations, and dirty crystal blooms—understated beauty. No spectacular, gift shop columns. No dramatic spires or ice-cream towers of water-smoothed flowstone—just insane limestone shards clinging, slipping, shifting underground; an ordinary cave. Joy, maybe, would have explored, but

I wasn't bold, like her. Instead, I tilted my head back, resting on my helmet, looked around and listened. Silence. During my downclimb, I'd been working too hard to observe the absence of sound. Now, at rest, I heard nothing at all, not one sound. No affectionate drumbeat pounded out by hands I almost knew, no laughter, no random half-caught words, no sirens, no electronic hum. Nothing sounded in this place.

I liked it.

*

The caving adventure started with drama, not calm—the entrance required a short downclimb, and as I moved into it, from above I heard branches snapping—looked to see Joy clearing brush from around her face. She squinted at me and cried out, "Juniper, there's a snake by your hand."

I narrowed my eyes like her, looking at my hand. Only leaves. *Shut up*, I wanted to tell her. *Don't see danger, and it won't see you*. I trusted her, but for the drive out here, I'd regretted their offer of a ride. I had wanted to think the day out for myself, without feeling trapped inside the stupid jokes and chatter in the vacuum of their backseat. Too bad for me; she saw into the leafage as well as she did logistics, because when I shifted my hand an inch to the left, I saw a flash of dry, patterned skin shift with me.

Solo, I never would have taken the time to find this place. Before I'd followed their bumper to dirt, still on the Interstate, the swerve and flow of traffic and high-tension talk kept my mind jumping, but on the dirt road, among trees and the occasional flit of animal movement, I had no padding against her expertise. She knew her stuff; it was the way she'd beat me over the head with it I couldn't abide, so much so that at the entrance, unwilling to wait for her, I started in the wrong way, holding myself outward with my arm wrapped around a limestone knob close to the nest of dry oak leaves where that snake lay coiled and silent. Having made my rotten choice, I stuck with it. I stopped when she yelled my name, but my body didn't react. "It's not rattling," Harsh muttered.

"You can see it too?" I asked, and as we spoke, my hand slid down the rock face, my foot found a lower hold. I skittered down, where there was no more rock and no more snake, jumping to the ground with muscle and earth reverberating in my knees.

"I couldn't do that. Just don't jump once we're inside," Joy said. Her knees were shot. High school team sports laid to rest at her adult doorstep—she moved in methodical, wary steps.

"Didn't want to wait." I smiled, dusting off my scraped palms, shaking off the downclimb sensation of loose gravel turning to water under my feet, then solidifying again.

"That wasn't the best way," Harsh said. "But it worked." Unwinding static rope, they descended west to avoid my east-dwelling snake. It was coiled, body tense and sleek, but no rattle sounded from within the leaves as we passed out of striking range. "Hope he's not there when we come out."

*

Caves breathe. Although Joy stopped scribbling our names in the exit log just inside the grate long enough to tell us that the shifts in air temperature and pressure along the first long passageway were carbon pressure from outside, they were, to me, exhalation. "The cave wants us to leave," I said.

Harsh laughed, but Joy said, "No, it's carbon pressure."

"So outside wants us to stay in?" I tried to keep it light.

She shook her head and pointed a gloved finger at the wall, where our headlamps lit up sections of muddy white mineral that sparkled, maybe with pyrite. "I think that's frostwork."

Harsh rolled his eyes, but she didn't see it. "Should we look at our route?" he asked. "Just make sure. Last time—"

"Oh, I know," Joy said, looking at me. "We looked for this place, but we didn't have any descriptions and we ended up on, like, three different routes. I mean, it was fun." She stopped looking at me, unfolding a scrap of paper from her pocket. "But we wasted too much time."

Harsh held her hand still and looked at the paper, scribbled with arrows and notes. "He said look for a huge mass of flowstone, like this—" she clicked through her camera. He nodded, and we started, Joy in lead. Her pace, steady without pause, granted permission to take in the descending landscape. The rippled panels of limestone wall gave way to slippery, round formations, undecorated, and difficult to hold.

"Three points of contact," Harsh reminded me when I slipped, and I pushed back against the rock, regaining balance. My steps tightroped from one firm place to another in a path as random as the arrangement of solid formations below our muddy boots. Although I wouldn't notice any soreness until a seemingly insane amount of time later, unknown muscles, core and limb, worked to maintain the pace and keep me stable between dark gaps of empty cave space. In the darkness, amid fluctuations in air weight and pressure, amid space where nothing contoured out into a palm or foot, we reached for every fraction of stability. Any one of us could fall. An injury could happen. Even with Joy's sense of adventure, and Harsh's geology degree, here, underground, amid this unreal accumulation of drips and pipes and stems and drabs of mineral earth, our collective plans and measurements and equipment could fall short. Our delicate, birdwing bones haunted my thoughts as our surroundings grew more otherworldly, my headlamp beaming white light across encrusted knobs, million-sided crystals, drip-thin pipes moistening into life from above and below. I felt panic rise, subside, and rise again.

Still. Their experience, not beauty, overrode my fetal worry. I followed, treading on moist rock without hesitation only because that was how they took in the cave, Harsh and Joy, as if its potential dangers were best overcome by turning a blind eye. I followed their lead.

From the start, we were bare-bones; three of us the minimum to safely enter. Although we didn't talk about who would do what along the way, someone would have to lead, another keep track of the thin strips of reflective plastic that marked our route, numbered in the dashed script of Joy's uncle, and a final person to remind everyone to take breaks, eat, and change batteries if any headlamps dimmed. For a second at the start, we fell into long-established outdoor roles—on hikes, I led, with Joy at my heels, cautioning me to find our path, at times correcting me. Harsh tailed. The cave, though, demanded hierarchy: Joy, whose uncle took her caving as a kid, took charge, leaving Harsh and I to trade spots in her wake. While the markers ran out, hundreds of feet and multiple turns between one and then next, he stopped us often, pointing out stunning, tiny deposits of growing stalactite or hollows of chiseled crystal encrustations. At first Joy would check her paper again, but then she tired of worrying her notes, angering or perhaps frightening Harsh, though we would each time arrive at the next, sequential number. Down, down into the dark, through markers three, and four, seven, nine, ten, the curious, faint Midwestern lilt of her voice and the caution in his Brahmin English enveloped me. I felt as if my own hungers were hidden, as were the other unpleasant aspects of our fractured, nature-obsessed lives.

Later on, when I would find a way to shed the day, our separation thirty feet past marker twelve would force slowness into my racing mind. Twelve and thirteen, I peeled delicately in my own mind, so as not to tear what lay beneath memory. It, twelve, my stopping place, was a stunning, small cavern below which lurked injurious, but not life-threatening, falls. Beyond us, at thirteen, the place where Harsh followed Joy into a challenge at which I balked, there was real danger. There, below a five-foot horizontal stem, the width of a body bent at the knees, there was such a long chasm that one slip could lead at worst to death, and at best to a three-day rescue that would endanger a whole crew. Traversing the unknown was an enduring habit between us, between me and my couple friends Joy Wells and Harsh Parikah. Together for sixteen years! What had I done for sixteen years, day in and day out? Brush my teeth?

Joy took the lead after twelve. Harsh had gone silent behind me, waiting, but Joy talked me forward into a tricky, twisting climb up to the chasm. While I rested, peering into the darkness, he lifted himself into the shadows behind me.

As soon as he'd entered the rest spot, Joy stepped out. She found her first hand- and foot-holds, lowered her body the foot-and-a-half downward, and placed her back against the opposing wall. Inch by inch, tension alone holding her safe above the abyss, she stemmed her way across.

Lot in her stead, I looked backward and saw Harsh close his eyes.

I would be unable to say, then as now, if I hated him for having the feeling that closed his eyes against her adrenaline urges, or if I wanted it for myself. I watched him watching Joy.

"The footholds aren't great," she said from the other side, sucking water and brushing strands of loose hair from her face, where they'd tangled in the straps of her helmet. Behind me, I could feel Harsh relax his hand against my hip, his breath close to my neck. Joy had tilted her headlamp into the dark space between that separated us from her. Even with a beam of light, all that was visible was narrowing, descending walls that swallowed the light. Her headlamp shone into the darkest stretch I'd yet seen—or maybe my imagination filled it in that way. Fear and black, who'd think?

I looked to the wall, tracing her route with my eyes but seeing nothing, and by the time she looked up at us, his body had already shifted perceptibly away from me. "If you fall—" she didn't end the sentence, but she was on the good side of it, smiling beneath her pale-blue helmet.

As if I'd disappeared, Harsh spoke. "I'm ready," he said.

I flattened against the rock, out of his way. At one time, Harsh was nobody in particular to me, an outdoor fiend like so many others. We'd rafted the Colorado together, all of us, and while he was never the first arrogant motherfucker to strip off his shirt and dive into the cold water, he was always there in the pack, until he wasn't *just* there. Watching him coalesce into a person in my life was terrifying—more terrifying than any life-or-death move I could make in nature. His hand brushing my hip, his breath close to my face.

As he stepped into the passage, I mimicked him, squeezing my eyes shut. But I couldn't. A love gesture felt like shit on me. I blinked open and watched him, mind dumb, seeing and processing nothing. Whatever Joy was to her boyfriend that made him unable to look when she crossed, and then follow her, they didn't look any more right than I felt at that moment.

For Harsh the traverse was easy. I'd meant to look for where his feet were going so that I could match his steps, and I caught the last stretch on to solid ground, but closing my eyes had cost me the chance to copy his first foothold—the crucial first step that sets the body up for success all the way across. I stared down at the rocks, trying to read them, to figure it out, wondering if backing away was failure to me. Was I giving up on myself, surrendering to the fact that this was my first time? Or that I didn't have Joy's fatalism, nor her patience. Or that my arm-span measured half of Harsh's. We'd compared them once, both holding out our limbs sideways like giant birds, forgotten by time and evolution. *Caw-caw,* someone in the group called out. Someone else laughed at us, but only Joy's laughter melted away the cocoon of her sleeping bag, and the sounds of wild night insects and curious mammals lost their usual rapture of meaning as our careless conversation wandered into intimacy right while she stared at us.

I don't know what we talked about.

I couldn't replicate it here.

Neither of us could undo our odd closeness, then—documented by Joy, looking at us, as if by accident, then smug. I had no idea what we looked like to her. Two people, I suppose. I think I meant to put the flat of my palm against her shoulder, to bring her close. I missed her, though, and smacked the tree beside us.

"Angry?" asked the guy who happened to be between our bodies.

"Could be," I said, staring at Joy as he passed into the night.

*

My headlamp was looking kind of brown, like the lights in our house when I was young and the electricity was about to conk out— "Goddamn Houston Power," my mom would say, slamming around into table legs and drawers until she found the flashlight, and there was never a time when she thought to put one in an easy-to-find place. Always the same routine. Waiting there in the dark, thinking of Mom, reminded me to conserve light. I fumbled with the headlamp buttons until I found the right combination of clicks to turn it off.

There, I found fear again: the darkest there was on earth, darker than anything, except, maybe, death.

That was the thing, after the silence. In that instant of shutting off my headlamp and plunging into the vastest absence of light I'd ever know, alive, it was not as if I'd closed my eyes or as if the power had gone on the fritz or even as if I'd gone under a wave, fifty yards from shore in some enchanted ocean. The cave dark into which I plunged when I turned off my headlamp was pre-nascent darkness, womb darkness, burial darkness, death darkness. The unmemorable past and the unknowable future reposed in the dark of a cave. Names raced through my mind: blood dark, like deep inside a heart, I thought too melodramatic; brain dark, like thoughts that never surface, too depressing; hard dark, like you can't see your own hand in front of your face until it brushes your nose, and even then it doesn't even feel like your own flesh because without seeing it you can't quite believe it exists—I like the sound of that one, but it felt ecstatic, and this darkest place was dreadful and broad and alluring. No transcending this.

For all it took me in, the darkness revealed nothing. I didn't come to Jesus or figure myself out—it was more like some holy, ultimate inner letting go, reckoning upon an absence I'd never known existed. For all I knew—*here*, said the universe to me. *Here's something you didn't know yet.*

But I knew too many things. I knew that being unfaithful meant, to me, that one person fails to abide by the rules of one relationship by joining another in a deceitful way. I knew that roles like leader and follower are harder to define when bodies conjoin than when they remain distant, and that after the loving starts deciding who led and who followed along is impossible because lovers are precisely those whose actions go unrecorded.

No inner truth hid in that dark, although I could not have avoided thinking about the three of us, alone down there. Joy and I, Harsh and I, they two together without me. I'm not wicked. Maybe I want to believe the thing I sought inside darkness was what we were rustling for in each other—realness, relentless, a thing striking none of us in our above-ground lives.

DON KUNZ

An Incident at Big Sandy Creek, 1864*

You woke in pre-dawn darkness, Cheyenne and Arapaho
Women worrying over old ones and children in your care,
Praying for your distant men hunting buffalo on the plains.
You emerged from lodges you had raised along the edges
Of a dry wash called Big Sandy Creek, breathed the chill of late
November, trudged beneath skeletal Cottonwoods through
Leaves kicked up by prairie wind like geese chittering,
Swirling, and falling to their deaths in time's repeating circle.
As dawn broke bloody above cooking fires, your eyes
Studied dust clouds rising on the horizon to the southeast.
You imagined buffalo. You, being hunted, thought of hunters.
You felt cold air like an approaching storm, heard thunder,
Then glimpsed Blue Coats riding, horses' hooves drumming.
You flinched at rifle fire ripping like lightning through clouds
Of black powder that dropped a stinging, blinding blanket of smoke
Across the remnant of land your men had not yet surrendered to Whites.

You watched your Peace Chief, Black Kettle, raise an American Flag
Above his lodge and White Antelope run toward the approaching riders
While waving a white shirt only to fall lashed by a lead rain.
Beneath Cottonwoods' long shadows, you ran northwest,
Women carrying old men and children up the widening creek bed.
You staggered through sand brown as the hide of tanned buffalo,
Used bare work-hardened hands to scratch beneath gnarled roots
Of Sandy Creek's ragged cutbanks shallow holes for hiding.
Colonel Chivington ordered his volunteer forces to chase you
Up both sides of the creek bottom and fire twelve-pound howitzers
Down into your screams. Shadows shortened, then fled into afternoon.
Your bullet-torn bodies became slippery with blood that spilled
Onto cold ground, nourishing thirsty sand and dead grass.
The shelters you dug in Big Sandy Creek became graves.

By mid-afternoon you had hurried homeless to relatives' lodges
In the Smoky Hill River country to the northeast or you had died.

Before supper the Blue Coats stripped you and scalped you,
Making your vulvas into hats, your sons' scrotums into pouches
They would parade through the dusty streets of Denver
And display in a local vaudeville theater like captured flags.

* On November 29th, 1864, the First and Third Regiments of the Colorado Volunteers
led by Col. John Chivington, the "Fighting Parson," made an unprovoked attack
on a village of mostly women and children, Cheyenne and Arapaho, camped in a
designated safe area for non-hostiles along Big Sandy Creek some twenty-three miles
northeast of what is now Eads, Colorado. Only Capt. Silas Soule and Lt. Joe Cramer
commanded their companies not to participate and later exposed the fight as the
"Sand Creek Massacre." In 1865 the incident at Big Sandy Creek became the focus
of one military and two congressional investigations. Each condemned Chivington
and his volunteers for cold-blooded murder. Chivington resigned his commission
and disbanded his regiments before they could be held accountable. No one was ever
prosecuted for participating in this mass murder.

RICK KEMPA

Grandma Sits Down

Her knees lean against the front of the battered old rocker,
getting their bearings, while she frowns out the window
at the garden, or squints into the poplars
to see if the sparrow hawks have returned. Slowly,
flat-footedly, like a mannequin in the department store,

she rotates, knees locked, keeping contact
with the chair. Her hands grope for, find, grip
the knobs at the ends of the wooden arms. She's not
looking at anything now, it hurts, she's concentrating.
Holding her breath like an astronaut, knuckles white

around the knobs, she lets herself fall.
The chair shudders, reels backwards, hangs
for a very long instant on disaster's rim—her eyes
are shut, head pressed back—and then begins to oscillate.
She breathes out: Another successful maneuver, nothing

to be especially pleased about. She knows
not to take for granted that she can get back up. Still,
the wind of her motion cools her cheeks. She continues
with the letter she's been writing: "The earth is beginning
to thaw. I am anxious to plant some seeds."

SCOT SIEGEL

The House on Willamette Falls Drive

—after the Blue Heron Mill closure, Oregon City, 2011

1. *Motive*
This was father's stronghold before the world took him
in a fit of orange soot, back-taxes, and Canadian whiskey.
Already checked-out at forty-two, he'd punch-in at the mill, half-
dead, reeking of chew and sweat. The goons at the Blue Heron
choked him with booze, turned him into a ghost before I could say
goodbye. Here is the anchor rope he taught me to grip when we'd fish
for black eels with bare hands from the rocks. She is my son he'd say
to the men, until the night I slept with a girl. She was old enough
to be my mother, but mother was a country where wars raged
and no children lived. Grandmother was no better; after
the principal tried to rape me, she blamed me for the hole
that was the pit of father's grief. But he and I knew that grief
was a hole below the murk of the mill, where the falls dissolved
in a dervish of mist, where the eels lived.

2. *Opportunity*
The laurels behind the house die back every June, and not for
a lack of rain. The chain-link below the road fell when the mill
burned. Now it reclines like a charred xylophone in a tangle of ivy.
Some nights I'm so lonely I walk the dike and play a jaunty tune
on my jew's-harp for that boy. I remember him screaming, thumping
the walls with his feet, calling me. He was still breathing when father
tried to lift him, but limp as a deadhead in the river. This is the anchor
rope father taught me to grip when they pushed the boy from the cliff.
That summer, sturgeon washed up on the shore, and we pickled them
for winter. But the flesh tasted like mud, and over the years father grew
ill; the mercury made him weep until his throat swelled and his mouth
bled. Now I half-sleep on his cot, under the trundle of compression
brakes; the jolt of axles over interstate potholes
reminds me of his hacking.

3. *Means*

I can still see father trying to save the whore as the men fled.
He was not like the others, would not leave her suffocating in a hall.
I can still see him silhouetted by the floodlight of a cop car, holding
a fillet knife to the light, when they kicked the door in. Even now,
it is hard to sleep. I have to touch myself until I feel a little seasick.
Then my eyes begin to close like this, and the world slowly dissolves
in the mist of the falls, and the house becomes an anchor rope again . . .
I don't have to tell the rest. He left no money, but taught me to fish
and fix old engines. Now I teach shop at the college where the mill
used to be. That '68 Mustang in the side-yard is mine, and the house
is nearly paid-off. The recession was rough—I had to cut down
on the Indian casino—but I'm doing just fine, no regrets,
and no intention of leaving, not as long as I've got this tape
of the principal and the boy, and a freezer full of eels.

PAULA COOMER

Basic Nostalgia

Just when you think you've got yourself pretty well put together, life comes along and smacks you upside the head with a baseball bat. That's me, or was me, and that baseball bat was the very unexpected and rather horrifying death of my father, who for reasons we still can't understand, decided on December fourth, 2015, to go out after dark, in the worst fog anyone can remember, to get the day's mail, a distance of several miles along narrow, loopy, and meandering southern Indiana back roads. Buffalo traces, those roads are called. He'd forgotten it, he told my mother, and he was worried about a bill that needed paying. My father hadn't driven after dark in years. He was strict about avoiding it. I told him it was an issue of those yellow-lensed glasses he so loved for the effect they had on the coloring of the landscape, but, as with so many things, he refused to listen, choosing instead to believe that he had developed night blindness in his old age.

The call came on December fifth, a Saturday, early in the morning. My brother. He's always the one to give me bad news, down to the 9/11 disaster. "This is the phone call you've always dreaded," he said. I immediately hung up on him. Couldn't breathe. He didn't have to say more. I knew. It was Daddy. My brother was right. I'd dreaded that phone call since the day I'd headed west from Indiana in 1977.

A cow pasture. Daddy had somehow launched his truck fifty feet across a ditch and plowed up a quarter mile of cow pasture. He'd managed to drag himself from the truck, pull himself some distance through the mud and manure, trying to get to help. How long? How long did he churn there on the ground, confused, panicked? How many times did he try to gain purchase by clawing at the closed door? My father's yellow clay-mud handprints on his black truck's door. My life is forever marked by those handprints.

Twenty-eight degrees. Four degrees below freezing. How long did it take him to succumb? And the poor farmer. Arrives at this pasture the next morning to find his cattle, forty or so of them, in Druid formation, standing around my father's body as if to protect it, to shield it from further onslaught by the elements. They did not disturb him, only watched over his body. One of the most moving things I learned is that a cow will lie down beside an ailing human, providing warmth until help arrives. None lay next to my father, nor were there fresh hoof prints nearby, which led the farmer and the police detective to believe he didn't linger long. We were comforted by the evidence of his struggle, however disturbing that image might be. To us the indication was that he died as he lived, his passion for survival prevailing as long as was bodily possible. Just as comforting was the fact that in the moments prior to his death, as his vehicle zoomed toward eternity, for a distance of fifty feet, he was airborne. He was afraid of airplanes, had never flown. Until the day of his death. Only coincidence that in the front seat of his truck, atop a stack of recent yard sale finds, was a jacket bearing the image of Superman, head on and in full flight, fist to the wind.

My husband, Phil, and I having oddly watched a show about the Donner Party two nights before. *Freezing to death.*

I always called him Daddy. Most people knew him as Red. Both names fitting for a man who was a cornerstone in so many lives. Everywhere we shared the news in his community, people shed tears. "I loved him!" was the most frequent response to the news of his passing. He was friend to many in his circuit of quick stops, fast food joints, various banks, gas stations, hardware stores, and, of course, the local post office. A storyteller. A charmer. I talked to him about every little issue. No matter how hard he might have been on me growing up, I saw him as my best friend, adviser, confidant, mentor. His was the genius of home-grown philosophy, one that included hard work and perseverance and an effort to look at the good in every situation. *"Turn around and face the monster,"* was his advice on walking through difficult times.

We were two peas in the family pod. People said we looked alike. I made it my business to pursue a life I thought he might have liked to pursue but could not because his twenties and thirties were squandered working two jobs in the support of me, my younger siblings, and our disabled mother. I knew Daddy wanted to be free. I cultivated that same desire in myself. We were, each in our own way, rebels. Outliers. Dreamers. We knew what it meant to see beauty in decay, to be at peace with the abandoned and unfinished, with some-day-some-time-some-place. We didn't see evil or sloth in procrastination but possibility, fomentation, percolation, preferring to place hope on the chance that a project left to mellow might grow into a more unique version of itself than if rushed or pushed toward a timeline. We both believed in giving creativity a wide berth.

My father's love of junk meant he saw beauty in places other people couldn't. Loved having piles of stuff around. He would have been a perfect candidate for a visit from *American Pickers*. Some of my favorite memories are of going to auctions and estate sales with my Daddy. Before his health started declining, that was our favorite thing to do. Having summers off as an academic allowed me to go home for two or three weeks every year. We would take off from the house almost every day, going to junk stores, auctions, and flea markets. We both had the same love for things old and dusty. I didn't care about buying stuff. I just wanted to be around the smells and the sounds and the people, looking at what others had cast off. The tang of rust still brings up the image of Choc-Ola and peanuts for me. Dad would buy a bag of roasted peanuts in the shell and eat them as he drove, tossing the shells to the wild. Choc-Ola was chocolate milk and seltzer in a bottle, and it was the yummiest accompaniment in the world to a country girl riding shotgun to the auction in whatever old car her Daddy happened to be driving at the time. There was always a rotation of junker vehicles around. If one wasn't running, another one was.

The journey east and then back west took thirty days and six thousand miles and featured dozens of stories that will take years to tell. A funeral, a house to empty, a mother to move. Too much to fathom, too much to digest. My siblings, mother, and I passed through the ceremony and the many tasks like seaweed through saltwater, drifting to what called us, what needed us, what hobbled us. So much work to close out the house of a sixty-year-marriage and a set of parents. My father saved every pay stub, every bank statement, every check, every utility bill—every piece of paper that proved he'd earned or paid or purchased something. Sixty-three years of it, from the time at the age of seventeen he walked off his own parents' homestead and took his first paying job. The work to sort through it all fell to me. Yes, mice. Yes, a few bugs. Not much in terms of assets. Plenty in terms of a life frugally lived yet with a clear penchant for minor risk-taking and exploration. For some reason an old TV cable bill from the 1980s caught my eye: he subscribed in those days to basic cable and the Nostalgia channel. That would have been two years after I left home for good. He loved old movies. Westerns. John Wayne. He loved to buy and sell. Loved cars. Coins. Knives. Tools. Property. Loved the idea of getting a return on his money. Small-time but busy, is how I would now describe my father's financial life.

He had already distributed some minor heirlooms to us children over recent years, so there was little I wanted to take with me, but I am so happy I got the cow bells from his family's old farm to remind me of the protective souls which watched over him in his last moments. A wristwatch from his working years, the crystal yellowed. A pair of drugstore eyeglasses. A money bag from Buffalo, Kentucky, once used by my grandfather to carry tobacco money after he sold the annual crop at the Burley warehouse. An auction ticket. Pages of notes in my father's hand: a land sale, a tornado, directions to the old family farm. A hickory walking stick he harvested himself. A set of crocks I scrubbed free of his and my mother's handprints and caked sugar. Photocopies of old photos. My father's family history. A sad tale of dead and orphaned children, mountain cabins, and wrongful decisions.

Both sides of the travel merged with gratitude for the fact that my husband and I had a dependable vehicle to drive and money enough to stay in decent hotels, eat nutritious food. I felt guilty being warm, riding in a comfortable seat, while Daddy lay cold on a coroner's slab. He always drove junkers, was always going out without socks or a coat, didn't care enough to clean his surroundings, house or vehicle. He could work on cars and trucks himself, at one time had nearly two dozen of them sitting around for spare parts, was working on the truck that carried him to infinity on the day before he died.

Twenty-one hundred miles in four days to get there: Washington, Idaho, Utah, Wyoming, Nebraska, Iowa, Illinois, Indiana. Add Kentucky, Tennessee, and North Carolina, to get my mother re-positioned at my brother's house. Then all those states in reverse again. Yellow line down the middle of so many highways, zip-zipping in time to my breath, my heartbeat, my spontaneous sobbing. My wish that the sinister nature of time could be sweetened, that I could have those carefree, healthy days of earlier years with my father back again. That there would be no diabetes, no heart disease. No slowly-evolving vascular dementia.

As if my father's death, closing down the house, and moving my mother to North Carolina from Indiana weren't enough, for some reason I agreed to be one of the executors of my father's will—a dogpile of paperwork. Dad left a stack of questions with few answers, and my brother and I were the only detectives. Signed, sealed, and deemed worthy by a judge in the state of Indiana. Because we were both from out of state, we had to put up a bond, just in case one of us decided to "make off" with the handful of one-thousand-dollar accidental death insurance policies we were charged with tracking, some older than I am. I called banks and insurance companies from my writing studio. Most of the stack of policies were dead as my father. The IRA's cashed in.

Voices at the other end of the phone offered condolences, but none of those insurance types could actually *believe* Daddy was dead until they had the paperwork to prove it. My choking voice wasn't enough. They wouldn't even send the forms to request the forms to submit a claim to insurance companies unless until we mailed a half-dozen proof-ful documents attesting to the fact that the man who walked me through the colicky night when I was a baby froze to death in a cow pasture exactly 4.2 months ago. Banks wouldn't say whether he had an account with them or not. Not until we mailed evidence of the judge having pounded the gavel that declared our father as vanished into stardust. Day after day and for weeks, I was forced to look at Daddy's death certificate, to handle it, to photocopy it. Looked at my name on his last will and testament. My mother's. My brother's. My sister's. The "we" that was we.

My brother, bless his heart, has the tough job. He and his wife are caring for our very disabled mother, who, if statistics bear out, we can also expect to leave us in the next few months. She's been waning since Dad died. ER visits. Antibiotics. Antidepressants. Bowel preparations. Pills to subdue her bladder. Pills to sleep. Pills to prevent her blood pressure from hoisting itself aloft. "The world is about waste management." This was my brother speaking, in a recent email. Our mother is now the complete and total focus of his and my sister-in-law's life. His calls leave me feeling helpless. I'm twenty-five hundred miles away. I don't know how to help. Every time the house phone rings I expect to hear the news. She's gone. Now Mom's gone, too.

A sad and difficult time.

Losing a parent changes you. No one tells you this. Even at nearly sixty years old, I could consistently feel in my day-to-day activities the protective spirits of my mother and father shrouding me, lightly but implicitly, even from twenty-one hundred miles away, even as they were nearing their eightieth birthdays. Only recently have I stopped feeling my mother's caring reach, which makes me think she may indeed be dwindling. Not having that sense of them has left within me resonating halls of vulnerability. Like all the ships suddenly left the harbor.

Like the Reevers are going to come chew me up any minute.

The night of Dad's funeral, my son Gabe, my husband Phil, and I went out to a place in Corydon, Indiana, called Point Blank Brewing Company, to do what any red-blooded human (except my parents) would do, and that is raise a glass (the southern pour is a real thing) to the most incredible human on the planet. I had been encouraged by a close friend to watch for angels and miracles during this difficult time, but I wasn't expecting to find Troubadours of Divine Bliss, a soulful, goosebump-producing duo from Louisville by way of New Orleans, one of whom passed by us during the break, close enough for me to mention how much I loved their music and for her to say, "You surely look familiar." I mentioned we were toasting Daddy, explained what had happened (auto accident, fog, freezing temps, cow pasture, etc.) only to have her say, "You've got to talk to my partner." The other gal came over and told her story of having lost her beloved father, also with diabetic dementia, two months prior to a hit and run accident. He was a pedestrian in a crosswalk one minute, a candidate for a coffin the next. Her words to me were, "Let this rip you open." I knew what she meant because I needed to be ripped open. I've been deeply angry for a very long time, mostly having to do with an estranged sister, my burdensome disappointment in the devolution of American academics, and, as a mere writing instructor, the devaluation of my part in it, and from which I'd departed myself in the spring of last year. I guess you could say I was flat angry over being me.

Then the Troubadours went back to the stage and said, "This one's for Albert and a tribute to an amazing man's passing," and proceeded to play this song they'd written called "Superman," of all things, about what it takes to earn the name Dad. Of course, my father's name was Albert (had I told them that? I certainly had not told them about the Superman jacket), so I bawled like a baby, right up until they said, "and here's a little more upbeat song for Albert," at which point they lapsed—unwitting—into my father's all-time favorite song, Johnny Cash's "Ring of Fire."

Superman kept showing up throughout that next week, and we all felt pretty strongly that, if there was any way possible, Daddy was reaching through the ether, trying to let me know he was okay. He had different ways to reach my siblings and mother, but this one was specifically for me. I always thought he was capable of anything. Clearly, he was.

I want to say I'm doing this well, this thing of getting on with life, but, my skills come and go. Sometimes I stare into space for long periods of time. Yesterday afternoon, right at three o'clock, I had the unpremeditated urge to go sit by the river. Phil was all for it. He got up, put his shoes on, and off we went. On the way, we saw a girl in a Superman shirt walking down the sidewalk. "There he is," Phil said, "making sure you know he's still with you. That must be why you wanted to go out."

Of course, I knew who "he" was. Happens randomly. I will suddenly have the urge to drive to a particular store or to carry out a neglected errand, and there will be that damned Superman image in some form. I've decided it's Daddy guiding me to make these spontaneous treks. It always seems to be on the days I'm missing him most.

CONTRIBUTOR NOTES

Contributor Notes

Betsy Bernfeld is a librarian and lawyer in Jackson Hole, Wyoming. Her anthology of historical Wyoming poetry, *Sagebrush Classics: Pure Wyoming Stuph*, was published by Media Publishing in Kansas City, Missouri, and her own poems have recently appeared in *Black Hills Literary Journal*, *Manifest West*, *Labyrinth*, a WyoPoets chapbook, and *Blood, Water, Wind, and Stone: An Anthology of Wyoming Writers*.

Paula Bramlett has spent her adult writing life supplementing curriculums with enrichment materials. Her engagement in historical research and interest in strong characters from the past serve as the core of her stories. "Annie Oakley" is part of a larger work-in-progress celebrating the cowgirl spirit of selected women honored by the National Cowgirl Hall of Fame.

Kierstin Bridger is a Colorado writer and author of two poetry collections: *Demimonde* (Lithic Press) and *All Ember* (Urban Farmhouse Press). She is editor of *Ridgway Alley Poems*, co-director of *Open Bard Poetry Series*, and co-host of *Poetry Voice Podcast*. She earned her MFA at Pacific University. Follow her at KIERSTINBRIDGER.COM.

Don Cadden and his wife Pam live in the mountains just south of Alpine, Texas. Don has produced two CDs of music and poetry, and a book, *Tied Hard & Fast—Apache Adams, Big Bend Cowboy*. He received the Heritage Award from the Texas Cowboy Poetry Gathering in 2014 for his commitment to Western life.

In her previous life before marriage, children, and a full-service restaurant, **Sally Clark** was a cowgirl. She now lives in Fredericksburg, Texas. Her award-winning poems have been widely published in journals, anthologies, magazines, and gift books. This is her second appearance in a *Manifest West* anthology. Follow her at SALLYCLARK.INFO.

Paula Coomer writes fiction, non-fiction, and poetry. She has authored seven books, including the novel *Jagged Edge of the Sky* and food memoir *Blue Moon Vegetarian*. Ms. Coomer lives near Hells Canyon in southeast Washington State, where she teaches writing, organizes writing retreats, and has completed work on a third novel.

David Lavar Coy, from Yuma, Arizona, remains a professor emeritus at Arizona Western College, and is former director of the Writing School there. He has been creating poems for nearly fifty years, some published in previous issues of the *Manifest West* anthologies.

Anita Cruse grew up in Durango, Colorado, where she still lives and attends Fort Lewis College, studying writing. She trains barrel racing horses and competes herself in the Four Corners area. Her work has previously appeared in *Labellum, The Independent,* and *Images.*

Carolyn Dahl was the Grand Prize winner in the 2015 national ekphrastic poetry competition, ARTlines2. Her writing has been published in twenty-five anthologies (including *Manifest West: Even Cowboys Carry Cell Phones*) and journals such as *Copper Nickel, Rock and Sling, PlainSongs,* and *Hawaii Review.* Carolyn is the author of *Transforming Fabric, Natural Impressions,* and co-author of *The Painted Door Opened: Poems and Art.* Follow her at CAROLYNDAHLSTUDIO.COM.

Debbie Day has always been passionate about writing stories and poetry. Her children's book, *Itchy Mitchie,* was published in March 2015 and her non-fiction short story can be found in *The Book of Hope* anthology (Silver Owl Publications, 2017). Follow her at DEBBIEDAYAUTHOR.BLOGSPOT.COM or on her Facebook page: DebbieDay Creations.

For thirty-six plus years, **Gail Denham's** poems, short stories, news articles, and photos have appeared in a wide range of publications—books, magazines, brochures, calendars. Denham's interests include family, humor, storytelling, and faith. Although retired, her writing continues. Denham and her husband have four sons and many grandchildren; a large part of Gail's inspiration.

Harrison Candelaria Fletcher is the author of *Descanso for My Father: Fragments of A Life* and *Presentimiento: A Life in Dreams*. His essays and prose poems have appeared widely. He teaches in the Colorado State University Non-fiction Program and Vermont College of Fine Arts MFA Program.

Corinna German writes creative non-fiction and poetry with the beautiful Absaroka-Beartooth Wilderness of Wyoming and Montana over her shoulder. She is a native of Gunnison, Colorado and is a life-long hunter and outdoor adventurer. Her work has recently appeared in *Blood, Water, Wind, and Stone: An Anthology of Wyoming Writers*.

Leah Hedrick is a current poetry student in Creighton University's MFA program in Omaha, NE. She received her BS degree from Purdue University in 2014. In addition to *Manifest West*, her work has appeared in *Columbia Poetry Review* and *NoiseMedium*.

Rick Kempa edited the anthology *On Foot: Grand Canyon Backpacking Stories* (Flagstaff: Vishnu Temple Press, 2014) and co-edited, with Peter Anderson, *Going Down Grand: Poems from the Canyon* (Fruita: Lithic Press, 2015). His latest poetry collection is *Ten Thousand Voices* (Oakland: Littoral Press, 2014). He lives in Rock Springs, Wyoming. Follow him at RICKKEMPA.COM.

Robert Kostuck is an M.Ed. graduate from Northern Arizona University. Recently published fiction, essays, and reviews appear in many American and Canadian print journals and anthologies. He is currently working on short stories, essays, and novels; his short story and essay collections seek a publisher.

Don Kunz taught literature, creative writing, and film studies at the University of Rhode Island for thirty-six years. His essays, poems, and short stories have appeared in over eighty literary journals. Don has retired to Bend, Oregon, where he is a member of the five-man, philanthropic High Desert Poetry Cell.

Annie Lampman is a creative writing professor at the Washington State University Honors College. Her writing has been awarded a *Best American Essays* Notable Essay, a *Pushcart Prize* Special Mention, first place in the *Everybody Writes* contest, an Idaho Commission on the Arts writing grant, and a national wilderness artist's residency through the BLM.

Lisa Levine's fiction has been published in *Furious Gazelle* and *Bird's Thumb*, which nominated her story "Shelter" for a 2015 Pushcart. She teaches creative writing at Southern New Hampshire University and holds an MFA from the University of Arizona. She writes eco-adventure and hyper-realistic fiction. Follow her blog at CARGOCOLLECTIVE.COM/ALLUVIALDISPOSITIONS.

Ellaraine Lockie is a widely published and awarded poet. Her eleventh chapbook, *Where the Meadowlark Sings*, won the 2014 Encircle Publication's chapbook contest. Upcoming is *Tripping with the Top Down* from Foothills Publishing, a collection of travel poems through the American West. Ellaraine teaches poetry workshops and serves as Poetry Editor for the lifestyles magazine, *Lilipoh*.

Jessica McDermott is a fourth generation Idahoan whose writing is heavily influenced by the culture and landscape of the West. She holds an MFA from the University of Idaho in Creative Non-fiction Writing and a BA in English and History from Utah State University. Her work can be found in *Animal: A Beast of a Literary Magazine, Apeiron Review, velvet-tail,* and *Green Panda Press.*

Cindy L. Prater lives in Northeast Nebraska with her husband, three grown children, and four sweet grandchildren. She drives eighty miles round-trip to teach special children. She writes when she can, tries to garden in sand, and is starting to think about retirement.

Riashantae Sides works at an Oregon community college that helps teenagers to finish high school. She and her husband have two young children, with a third on the way. Riashantae's experiences with people, nature, and faith inspire her poetry. She intends to continue writing as part of her lifelong journey.

Scot Siegel is a poet and land-use planner who has worked with small towns and cities throughout the western United States. His most recent books of poetry are *The Constellation of Extinct Stars and Other Poems* (2016) and *Thousands Flee California Wildflowers* (2012), both from *Salmon Poetry* of Ireland. His work has appeared in *Manifest West, High Desert Journal, San Pedro River Review,* and *Terrain.org,* among others. Follow him at SCOTSIEGEL.COM.

Kathleen Winter's collection *Nostalgia for the Criminal Past* (Elixir Press) won the Antivenom Prize and Texas Institute of Letters first book award. Her poems are forthcoming in *AGNI, Michigan Quarterly Review, Prairie Schooner, Yale Review,* and *32 Poems.* She received fellowships from Dobie Paisano Ranch, Dora Maar House, James Merrill House, Cill Rialaig Retreat, and Vermont Studio Center.

About the Staff

Sheena Feiler is a Colorado native who lives in the Vail Valley. She graduated from the University of Colorado with a BA in English Literature and is a graduate of Western State's Publishing Certificate. During her participation in the Publishing program, she worked as an editorial intern for Conundrum Press in Golden. Currently, Sheena works as a freelance editor and writer while she enjoys the mountain life.

Sapphire Heien is a freelance editor and writer who lives in Laramie, Wyoming, with her husband Jeremy. She holds a Graduate Certificate in Publishing from Western State Colorado University and a Bachelor of Arts in English and Professional Writing from the University of Wyoming. Her essays have won multiple national and international awards and placements from such institutions as the Ayn Rand Institute, Bill of Rights Institute, and American Foreign Service Association, and her articles and short stories have been published in the *High Plains Register, Starsongs, Home School Enrichment*, and *Oakwood*.

Elizabyth A. Hiscox is the author of *Reassurance in Negative Space* and *Inventory from a One-Hour Room*. She holds an MFA from Arizona State University, and a PhD from Western Michigan University, where she served in editorial positions for *Third Coast* and *New Issues Poetry and Prose*.

Caleb J. Seeling is the Director of the Certificate in Publishing at Western State Colorado University. He began working in publishing in 2006 and founded Samizdat Publishing Group in Denver in 2009. The company has since expanded, forming two imprints (Conundrum Press and Samizdat Creative), publishing between twenty-thirty books each year. An active member of several publishing and arts organizations, Caleb is also a social entrepreneur, finding ways to serve the greater community and disadvantaged youth through strategic partnerships.

Mark Todd is Editor-in-Chief at Western Press Books and has taught at Western State Colorado University since 1988. He's author of seven books: two collections of poetry, a science fiction novel, and co-author with wife Kym O'Connell-Todd of the paranormal comedy Silverville Saga trilogy, as well as a creative nonfiction book on haunted hotels.

Sonya Unrein is a freelance editor and book designer. She has a master's degree from the University of Denver in Digital Media Studies, and lives near Denver with her husband and cat.